"*The Directory of Northwest Intuitive Arts Practitioners* is much more than a guidebook. Cindy Evans takes you through the infinite variety of healers and intuitives available, including helpful interviews, detailed listings on services, and all the other information you need to find exactly the right counselor, psychic, shaman, dream worker, clairvoyant, healer and energy worker for you."

Alice Anne Parker, author of
Understand Your Dreams and
The Last of the Dream People

The Directory of Northwest Intuitive Arts Practitioners

The Directory of Northwest Intuitive Arts Practitioners

C. L. Evans

Trumpet Vine Press
Portland, Oregon

First Trumpet Vine Printing: October, 1998.

Trumpet Vine Press
Portland, Oregon
(503) 591-9819

Dedicated to Mike,
who has given me a lifetime of love.

Acknowledgments

This book was a blessing to me in many ways, not the least of which was the fact that some wonderful people contributed their support to it.

I am first and foremost grateful to Hope Hadley, without whose friendship and support this could not have been written. It was during a get-together at Hope's house that the idea of the Directory was first conceived, and she has been a huge help to me in both tangible and intangible ways.

I am also grateful to BJ Schmeltzer, Carole Sletta, Shirlee Teabo, Nancy Milliman, Nancy Howard, Dianne Geldon, Susan Keiraleyn, and Miriam Selby, all of whom contributed their time and expertise to the making of this book.

Contents

Introduction

How This Book Came to Be

On a cold February evening about a year and a half before publication of this book, I was visiting with a group of friends and speculating on how nice it would be to get a group reading. Despite our interest in metaphysics, we realized that among the four of us, we knew of only two or three practitioners in the area. We had not visited these practitioners and all we knew about them was what could be described in a small ad.

Out of that conversation came this *Directory*. For a year, I visited clairvoyants disguised, as I like to say, as a regular customer. Although I had visited psychics once a year just for fun since 1978, I wanted to get oriented to what the majority of practitioners did and sort through the information in a more analytical mode. From that, I developed some strong feelings on courtesy, ethics and what genuine talent looks like.

After that year of investigation, I went back to the intuitives whom I felt were genuinely talented and asked them to be in this book. Then—and this is equally important —I asked them for names of other practitioners who were genuinely talented whom they felt should be included in the book. The result is a *Directory* that covers two states, as well as practitioners who regularly visit the Northwest and/or accept requests for readings from Northwest residents.

This brings up two issues: if someone's not listed in this book, does that mean they're not talented? The answer is a resounding no. Some practitioners had personal reasons for not wanting to be listed in this year's edition, such as pregnancy and subsequent child care demands. One individual declined to be listed because she was making a name for herself in another profession, and the knowledge that she was an intuitive would work against her in her job. Others were unable to get their information to me before publication deadline. There are others, especially in the more remote areas of the Northwest, whom I have not had the opportunity to contact up to this point. *The Directory of Northwest Intuitive Arts Practitioners* will be published every fall, with updated information, and hopefully we'll be able to include these individuals in our next edition.

The second issue is: does a listing in this *Directory* constitute some sort of seal of approval? Again, the answer has to be no. There is no federal or state licensing of psychics, healers and shamans in the United States. And to the best of my knowledge, neither is there a peer review board or self-governing body or any sort. For myself, I had neither the time nor the expertise to evaluate any practitioner in such a way as to guarantee that s/he would give consistently accurate readings, perform effective healings, or what have you. As a result, this Directory is meant only as a source of information from which an individual may make a more informed decision about which practitioner to visit, if any.

With that in mind, let's see who's who and what's what in the Northwest metaphysical community.

How to Get the Most
from Your Visit

To know if you've gotten what you want, you have to start out by knowing what you wanted in the first place. So it's a good idea to be clear on why you're contemplating a visit to an intuitive arts practitioner. For demonstration purposes, we'll assume you're making a visit to a psychic.

There are generally four reasons an individual visits a psychic:

1. **Curiosity.** What's a visit to an intuitive like, anyway?

2. **A desire to know the future.** This is particularly appealing if our immediate future involves the possibility of making some major changes. The majority of questions a sensitive is asked revolve around the future of money, love and health.

3. **Entertainment.** A visit to a psychic can be fun. And, let's face it, it's not very often we get a chance to hear someone talk to us about ourselves for a whole half-hour or hour.

4. **Spiritual Growth.** Many intuitives can provide amplification for that "still, small voice" inside us that guides us towards fulfilling our mission in life.

Okay. So now you know why you're contemplating a visit to an intuitive arts practitioner. Now how do you go about choosing one?

The best way, of course, is to get a recommendation from friends. Barring that, the second best way is to read the information in this book and then call the practitioner whose description of their work appeals to you. During the conversation, note how you feel. If there's a high comfort level while the practitioner is talking with you, go ahead and make the appointment.

How to Make the Most of Your Visit

When you're visiting a psychic for the first time, there are some concrete things you can do to get the most out of your visit.

First and foremost, be centered and receptive. On your drive over to the reading, do whatever you usually do in the way of focusing your energy and attention. Concentrate on what questions you would like answers to. If you believe in a Higher Power, ask that all information that you receive be to the highest good for all concerned. Take a few deep, slow breaths. Make sure you're as physically comfortable as you can manage: well-rested, reasonably fed, no alcohol or recreational drugs.

Knowing a little about what lies ahead of you will help to reduce your nervousness and increase your receptivity. Below is a description of what you can reasonably expect to happen at your reading.

First Contact.

Generally what happens is this: You hear about a good psychic from a friend, the Yellow Pages, or this book. You call, and most likely leave a message on an answering machine. You leave your name and phone number, and say that you are interested in a reading.

If the psychic has good business sense (incidentally, there seems to be no direct connection between business sense and psychic gifts or lack thereof), your call will be returned within 24 hours. (But two of the most gifted psychics I know have the business sense of a turnip, so keep in mind that the return call may take anywhere from an hour to two weeks.) When the psychic returns your call, they will give you a choice of options in terms of what kind of reading you can choose from and what length of time you would like the reading to last.

The intuitive will not only tell you what's on the menu, but they will also tell you the prices. They might say something like, "A half-hour reading will cost you x number of dollars, and that includes a life reading and three follow up questions that you can call in in within the next three months," or some such thing. Once quoted, the rates are firm. Not one single psychic I went to encouraged me to extend my visit and spend more money than we had originally agreed on.

What does a "typical" visit look like?

Okay, you've agreed on a time for your visit to your practitioner, and you drive out to their place of business. It may be their home or it may be an office. But wherever it is, it will more than likely be a cheerful, well-lit room with comfy chairs. A bit like a psychologist's office. I recommend you show up at least a few minutes early, not only out of common courtesy but also to calm your nerves. To the degree that you fear the unknown (and who doesn't?), you will have some apprehension about what you might hear in the next half-hour or hour.

You will be met by the intuitive, who will invite you to sit opposite them, again, in comfy chairs in a well-lit room. Like any two human beings, you two will make a few minutes of small talk as you get yourself comfortable, discussing things like the weather, whether you had any difficulty finding the place, that sort of thing.

Since it is your first visit to this particular practitioner, they will spend a few minutes telling you (1) what method or modalities they will use to access the psychic information they are about to relay to you; (2) what parameters they have, (for example, not giving lottery numbers), and (3) best of all: what their own attitude is towards the information they are about to impart. This, more than anything else, gives you your first insight into your psychic's personal worldview and how that will color the information. My favorite attitude was summed up by psychic Don Clarkson, who said, humorously, "I'm not the voice of God." Don is an urbane and witty man, and his perspective on psychic information is nicely balanced between the practical and the mystic.

Then we come to the meat of the matter. For the next 15 minutes or half-hour or whatever block of time you've reserved, the psychic relays to you the information they receive from their source. Generally, this information is given in a normal tone of voice, with the psychic looking you in the eye. Occasionally they will close their eyes to better focus on the information. But overall, a psychic reading usually looks like two friends sitting across from each other chatting.

Regarding tape recordings: Most of the psychics I visited encouraged tape recordings, although a small minority did not allow recorders at all. To get the most out of your reading, however, I strongly recommend that you be allowed to tape record it. There are several reasons for this. The first is that it's virtually impossible to remember everything that was said to you word for word, and listening to the recording will help you remember the information later. The second reason is that you will probably be a little nervous during the actual reading and you will want to listen again to what the psychic had to say when you are in a calmer and more receptive frame of mind. And finally, listening to your recording helps you to discover the multitude of layers of information that are contained in every reading.

At the end of the reading, your intuitive arts practitioner will ask you if you have any questions. Once the remainder of the session is concluded, you hand the psychic a check or cash, and then you leave. From here, my strongest advice is: go home. You've usually been given a lot to think about, and you're going to want to mull things over. You may even want to listen to the tape of the session again right away, although I personally prefer to let it sink in a bit.

Here some remarks are due about courtesy. Under no circumstances should you allow a psychic to be rude to you. In my experience, this has only happened once, and I was caught completely by surprise. (That person, I'm happy to say, no longer practices in Portland area.) You, as the client, should not be spoken to with disdain, abruptness, or anger. The psychics I visited for the purposes of this book, however, were unfailingly courteous.

The same is true from the opposite direction. You yourself should be courteous to the intuitive you are visiting. If the professional you're speaking with tells you that you're not going to win this week's lottery, don't try to bully them into making them tell you news that you'd rather hear. Accept any disappointing news with courtesy and as much detachment as you can muster.

How much should you tell a psychic?

It's best that you tell a psychic as little as possible. You don't want to contaminate what they're seeing with what you're only hoping they're seeing.

A psychic will ask you some basic information which you will readily want to give. Most will ask you your name and date of birth. They may ask you what area of your life you would like to focus on in the reading: career, health, personal life. Some will ask you to have questions written down, and that's a good idea in any reading.

My requests were usually for a general reading. You might phrase it as, "What does the Universe have to tell me?" At times throughout the reading, the intuitive may pause and ask you a question such as, "Does what I'm saying make sense to you?" After answering yes or no, you are free to elaborate or not, as you choose. These are all legitimate questions. As a general rule, though, the more specific your initial question is, the more specific the psychic's answer will be. Strong feelings that you have regarding the question will also help the practitioner hone in on what needs to be told to you.

But there are, we might say, illegitimate questions. In my 20 years of visiting psychics around the country, I have been fortunate in only running into two or three charlatans, and they were the most likely to spend 20 minutes getting information from me. One was a woman in a small Southern California town who described herself as a channeler. When we first sat down together, she peppered me with detailed questions about my life. What did I do for a living? What did my husband do for a living? Did I have children? Describe the entire problem I was going to ask about.

Being young and inexperienced, I answered the questions as asked. In retrospect, I should've simply followed my instincts and called the whole thing off. But I wanted to give this woman a chance, and she had, after all, come recommended.

Then before the actual reading, while she was explaining her methods, she emphasized that my own subconscious already knew all the answers to my questions, and that the Universe couldn't tell me anything I already didn't know. After that, she began "channeling": still seated, she swayed slightly from side to side, eyes closed. Her voice became nasally. Then she began repeating back to me, in contorted syntax, exactly what I had told her earlier about the situations she had questioned me about. She gave me no additional information whatsoever.

Well, we live and learn. I'm still in the process of learning about the metaphysical community, but in the meantime I can at least share what I've picked up so far. This book is designed to help you avoid the kind of disaster I just described. There can be no guarantee of success, of course. A reading may be inaccurate for any number of reasons, but that's the risk you take in such a subjective field. But you can at least go into a session as fully informed as possible, and that is the mission of this book.

A Word About Professionalism

A gift for healing or intuition is a talent unto itself and does not necessarily connect to other areas of a person's character. Being an intuitive arts practitioner doesn't necessarily make an individual more spiritual, more intelligent, or more businesslike than, say, the average person on the street. Consequently, there is a wide range of professionalism among practitioners which has nothing to do with the efficacy of their services. In some cases, you are going to need to decide for yourself how important professionalism is to you versus how effective your practitioner is. Under the listing of professionalism, I include things such as:

Returning Your Call. How long does it take to return your phone call? If it's going to take more than 24 hours to get back to you, that information should be indicated in the pre-recorded message.

Punctuality. How long, if at all, are you kept waiting once you've arrived for your appointment? More than 10 or 15 minutes past the designated time is unacceptable.

Recordings. Does the reader provide their own tape recorder and tape? If not, that information should be conveyed to you on the phone so that you can bring your own.

Privacy. Is the session uninterrupted? Your practitioner should not be answering the phone or the doorbell once the two of you have sat down and begun the appointment. Family members or co-practitioners should not be wandering within hearing range of your session.

Payment. Do they accept checks or credit cards? Preferably, they do. If not, that information needs to be conveyed to you over the phone while you are setting up your appointment.

Compassion. Are they non-judgmental? You are allowing them to access private areas of your life. That privilege should not be abused, and that means that the psychic should convey the information with a compassionate and non-judgmental attitude. Neither should they give you advice in a manner you find pushy or condescending.

Integrity. Did they conduct the session as they described it to you over the phone? In other words, if you reserved a half-hour, did it last the full half-hour? Did they focus their information on the areas you two had agreed on at the outset of your reading? Ideally, they gave you more information than you requested.

Fee. Did you end up spending more money on the session than you had originally intended? Once you have agreed to a set amount of time and money, under no circumstances should the psychic try to persuade you to pay more money for more time in this particular session. They may suggest that you come back, however, and that may be appropriate. But go home and think about it before you agree to another appointment, so that you're not swayed by a practitioner who may be preying on your fears.

Confidentiality. Do they gossip about other clients by name? Again, you are allowing this person access into private areas of your life. If they tell you confidential information about other clients, what's to prevent them from revealing information about you inappropriately?

Profiles in Intuitive Artistry

Following are a few of the intuitive arts practitioners whom the author has visited. They have consented to be interviewed for this book.

Vivian: Helping Children Develop their Gifts

"I've worked with children of all ages"

"I insist that they have at least a healing relationship with their families."

"The children are very telepathic and they know it; we're the ones who don't know it."

Vivian Christianson has long recognized the intuitive talents of youngsters, and for good reason. She was raised with the kind of openness and nurturing that fostered her own natural abilities.

"I was raised by my godparents; one of them was from Hawaii and the other one was from the Philippines. There's a more charismatic openness to spirituality in those countries," Vivian explains, "so for us to walk to [Catholic] church every day and do our prayers and light candles for healing, this was a way of life for me."

Christianson's godparents did not discourage her from recognizing the validity of visions. "I always saw my guardian angel as a child. When you're being raised that way, you're not told that you don't. You're told every day that you do."

A love of nature combined quite easily with the mysticism of Christianity, and Vivian has precious memories of her childhood. "They had this beautiful, big, large garden area," she says of her godparents' home "and they taught me to speak directly to God and to speak directly with the Virgin Mother and the angels. So there wasn't separation there for me. I didn't understand," she continues, "when I got older why some religions would say you could only talk to God through Jesus Christ or all these boundaries that were put on with angels and things. I didn't have those boundaries."

From this organic background, teaching children to accept their natural abilities became something for which Christianson developed a passion. "When I was down in Salem, I formed a community group of young people. We brought in speakers on all the different topics so that they could start to get good, solid information."

Vivian teaches adults as well as children, and realizes that, for intuitives and healers, life is a lot easier when the training comes early. "I help people develop their own gifts and show them how to use them," she explains. "But before you've matured and learned to focus that gift, it's usually like a whirlwind because it's so unfocused and hard to channel."

In her classes, Christianson encourages a balanced lifestyle and discourages any tendencies to escape from everyday difficulties into the more welcoming realm of the spiritual. "If you're not dealing with something emotionally," she asserts, "you need to. You need to look at what's in there, because under that blocked emotion is your true gift.

"I want my students to live life in a direct manner. I don't want them to hide from their challenges. I don't want them to pretend that [the problems] are not there; I want them to embrace them.

"So when I teach, I teach that you must fully live within the four quadrants: your spiritual world is only 25 percent of your world. The other three are the physical, the emotional and the mental. And that will create the balance within your being.

"And I'm really specific," Vivian emphasizes, "in that they don't get to run away from the issues of their own family; that all of them have to have good relationships, or at least healing relationships with their own families. They come from wonderful families," Christianson explains. "These aren't kids that had bad families and needed someplace. These are kids that have really good families and were too gifted and the explanations weren't there that made sense within them."

Not surprisingly, Vivian has a lot of love for the students she has mentored over the years. "I have a beautiful extended family," she says, referring to her students, "and I feel very blessed that these young people have stayed very close to me over the years and participate as an extended family.

"I know that I'm doing what I came here to do. And that is incredibly rewarding; I love that."

Goal: Client Empowerment

Mark Dodich leads people to open their own Akashic records

"My philosophy of life is we are in this big shift of change," explains Mark Dodich, "whatever you want to call that. In my opinion we're in a place in this world where people need to be choosing to live in their truth. My role is to work with those people who are trying to get themselves across that bridge into a higher level of truth."

Mark is trying to explain to a questioner the difference between a psychic reading and spiritual work.

Dodich uses the term "psychic reading" to describe a more workaday type of intuitive experience. "I consider the psychic to be working in this temporary kind of energy such as, 'If you keep on this path, you're going to meet Bob or Mike.' I call it phenomenal or an event-oriented type of reading.

"Sometimes you need to do that," Mark explains, "because if you see somebody driving towards a cliff you'd want to tell them to take a left; so you need to do that to help them over the bridge."

Mark continues earnestly, "But you don't want to just leave it there; you'd want to go to the next level of, What is the meaning? How can you work through this self-worth or this judgment or whatever the issue is, to help them see that they really are in control? And that for me is going to the more spiritual level, which is where I focus all my work. And truly, when you do that kind of work it's far easier and it's far more rewarding."

Easier? "Oh, it is. Because that psychic energy drains you. Whereas — this is my definition, mind you — with that spiritual energy, you're going directly to the Source and calling that information.

"I do a little prayer before I give every consultation," says Dodich, "and I take that person to the core of the universe and open up that door of information, the Akashic records or whatever you call that source of oneness. I take them there and have them open that door too, so that they know they are empowered in bringing forth what they're bringing forth, and that I'm just kind of like this radio receiver that translates it for them.

"Whether they're doing it for themselves, or they're going out to actually be teachers doesn't really matter so much. The point is they're choosing to live their truth."

Dodich has known material abundance and he has known spiritual abundance. He likes both, but knows the price of sacrificing one for the other. "In San Francisco I was this rising star young businessman, selling aluminum all over the northwest part of the country," he recounts. "It was this real ego trip; I had my suits made in Hong Kong and I was going to eat in the best restaurants at the top of whatever the bank building happened to be downtown, and it was a pretty nice lifestyle. Listening to this comfortable, low-key, articulate gentleman, an observer could easily see how he could attain a lifestyle that included the best of everything. But somewhere along the way, he realized that the material goods weren't filling the void.

"But I had gotten more into meditation," he continues, "and the astrology, of course, had continued to progress. But I was trying to change my habits. I used to drink a lot as a businessman, and I decided that drinking is killing me; I've got to find other activities to do on the weekends.

"I ended up going to this crystal healing lecture before they were popular." The lecture was being presented by Frank Alper, who was connected with the Church of Tzaddi (which is out of Boulder) and Arizona Metaphysical Society, which is out of Phoenix.

"I laid [down] in a pattern of these 12 gigantic crystals and I could feel it," recalls Mark. "I'm pretty skeptical, so when I can feel it, I knew there was something here."

The effect of the lectures and crystals was profound. "Over the next four or five years — between being transferred by the company and job-hopping for better jobs and what have you — I followed a ministry program through the Church of Tzaddi." Tzaddi, Mark explains, means brotherhood or universal brotherhood. "It was basic metaphysical training: channeling before channeling became popular; it was hands-on healing, a lot of Cabalistic things."

After receiving his ministry license, Mark left his cushy corporate job and began his lifework in earnest: that of helping his clients use their daily experiences to reach to a deeper truth. In the beginning, there were many questions. "How do you get past somebody's blocks? Or how do you take them over that bridge from the quick answer they're looking for to recognizing that, 'Gee, you've been in this relationship 12 times over the last 30 years, it's just been with different names and different faces, but it's the same relationship.' How do you get through to help people see that instead of just wanting to create the same thing over again?"

In the process, he learned to be non-judgmental, and
to guide his clients toward "stepping into their natural
spiritual state" rather than encouraging a dependence on
him. "In that way you're helping to empower these people,
rather than create greater addictions in them," Dodich
believes.

Preparing Us for the Energy Shift

Eighth Generation Reiki Master Teaches Us How To Make Our Physical Form and Consciousness More Permeable

"This isn't something that's going to happen; we're in the process of it."

So states Alice Anne Parker, described in *Honolulu Magazine* as one of Hawaii's best-known psychics.

"There's something going on that's so profound I am just barely able to capture it," relates Alice Anne. A soft-spoken and articulate woman, this Phi Beta Kappa graduate of Hunter College sits in an island of calm amidst a lively Starbuck's while she explains earth changes.

"I can feel it," she says. "Gravity is getting weaker; the pulse rate of the earth is increasing, and those are going to come together."

She believes that Reiki is one good method for adapting with the earth to its changes in vibrational frequencies.

"One of the reasons that I'm teaching Reiki to people is that when you start doing Reiki healing on yourself every day, something that is seated in the DNA is starting to open up. I believe that that needs to happen in order for us to endure the energetic shift that's going on; it's healing at a cellular level."

Another group whom Alice Anne recognizes as already vibrating on a different level are Aborigines, a group she visited some years ago.

"When you shake hands, they're vibrating differently," she notes. "It's almost like it's water. It's like your hand might just go through, even though they're really strong.

"It's not faster or slower; it's just different. It's like music that's in 4/4 time and music that's in 3/4 time. One might be the same speed as the other, but the rhythmic beat is different. It's a different rhythmic field they're in."

Alice Anne likens her quest for teaching these vibrational techniques to planting seeds. "It's not really healing; it's almost like fertilizing. It's like you're fertilizing something energetically so that you can adjust physically and move to a less dense material level." Her clients, she notes, are from many countries and the majority of them have no interest in metaphysics.

"They're businesspeople," she remarks. "I have a lot of clients in Hawaii who are attorneys. I have a client in Greece who's a trader." Parker gives Reiki intensives throughout the U. S. and Europe. "So I'm engaged in that. I'm also forcing, cajoling, getting as many people as possible to learn that, or something like that."

Does Parker feel that this change in vibrational frequency will affect land masses and weather? "I'm not worried about that," she responds. "Something's breaking apart very rapidly and it's a good thing; it's not a bad thing. It's not like, 'Oh, God, California falls into the ocean.' That's a translation into physical terms of something that is energetic."

She predicts, however, that Y2K, the problem of computers being unable to read the year 2000 in their programs, will cause some chaos.

"I was looking at some dates, and it looks like they're kind of waves. Like there's a wave in May of 1999, the first big one.

"There's one possibly around April 7 or end of April," she continues. "Then a stronger possibility in May. And then it looks like about five waves where a whole worldwide grid goes down, and then they get it back.

"So, it looks like it runs until about late spring, 2000, and then things are back in place. So there's about a year and a half of recurring chaos. That's my sense of it right now."

But Parker does not foresee helplessness as a response to a year and a half of rolling shutdowns. "I have faith in people's ability to adapt.

"And," she adds practically, "I'm getting a generator."

Shirlee Teabo: A Voice for Ethics

Long-Time Psychic Urges Integrity, Responsibility

"You have to have a feeling of responsibility — when the person's there as well as when they leave. Because people will change their lives on the turn of a card."

During her three decades as a psychic, Shirlee Teabo has seen public acceptance for practitioners rise dramatically. Bookstores, for example, confined metaphysical books to small, remote shelves labeled Occult. In many states, it was against the law to practice "fortune-telling."

This decade, however, has seen an interest in metaphysics unlike any since the rise of Spiritualism in World War I. Psychic fairs, Whole Life Expo, metaphysical books and catalogs are raking in the big bucks. And along with this blossoming of interest in spiritual growth has come a need for self-discipline and caution.

"About 28 years ago, there weren't many people around," comments Shirlee on the number of practicing psychics. "But what's been alarming and gratifying, both, is how it's totally acceptable now to the point where it's almost a dangerous kind of a thing."

Dangerous? "Because everybody and his brother, without any training, without any character development of their own, are out there. I've had people terribly exploited.

You can be the best psychic in the world," Shirlee explains, "and be a total rotter. Charles Manson's a very good example of this. Adolph Hitler is another one. People will use their psychic ability almost as a recruiting thing to get people to follow their spiritual path, doing what religion's been doing forever, causing inner fights and things like that."

Teabo feels that any intuitive arts practitioner has an ethical responsibility towards the client. "In this kind of work, it's very important that you have, first of all, your own life in order. If you don't have your life in order," she emphasizes, "you shouldn't be in this kind of work."

An earthy and outspoken woman, Teabo has strong feelings about keeping focused on the highest good. "If you really want to develop in this work — I know this sounds funny — keep your innocence. That doesn't mean be gullible. But, you know, keep your innocence so that you stay clean.

"Also, you have to be able to stay centered," she continues. "And you can't be judgmental, because you're going to see and hear things that are totally against your own belief system."

Shirlee herself is direct and unpretentious, and is quick to express a similar preference for the kinds of readings she receives. "Whenever I go to another town, I love to visit a psychic," she comments. But I don't like the trappings, like when you go into a place, there's steam and all that kind of garbage. And they should be able to speak the language of the person," she continues, "not some metaphysical b.s. There shouldn't be a bunch of mystery."

In Teabo's experience, most people don't know how to look for an intuitive arts practitioner. In her seminars and lectures, she stresses that the most effective method is word-of-mouth; "ask around for a recommendation." If your friends and acquaintances don't have the information you need, she asserts, using *The Directory of Northwest Intuitive Arts Practitioners* is a good alternative.

"They don't know how to look," she explains, or what to look for. "Sometimes people visit a psychic because it's an 'in' thing. Sometimes it's because there are really problems.

"I don't want to be a therapist to people," Shirlee states. "But sometimes they just need a road map. I think they're looking for validation of their own judgment, and we're sort of like the American Automobile Association.

"You know you're going to take a trip, but we can sometimes tell you the easier road to get to."

Animals Take On Our Ailments So We Don't Have To

A Gift of Unconditional Love

During her years as an animal communicator, BJ has had some surprising experiences: she has communicated with mammals, fish and even spiders. And while all of these interactions carried their own gift of love and acceptance—even the spider—the highest level of unconditional love has come from those animals who willingly take into their own bodies the ailments that originated in the bodies of their owners. To some, it may sound unbelievable, but BJ has seen enough of these instances to realize that it's more than just coincidence.

"I was called out to a big stable here on the Oregon Coast to walk through and give 10-minute readings on all the horses," recounts BJ. "I noticed this one particular horse— it's a black horse—and he's got a wrap on his left rear leg. And so I asked the owners, 'What's with the wrap?'"

"Oh, that's an old thing," she said dismissively.

Following her instincts, BJ persisted. "I think we might want to talk about this. I feel like we really need to. It feels like this has something to do with the family," she continued. "Do you have children?"

The owner replied that she had two boys, ages nine and six.

When asked about the history of the horse's injury, the owner recounts, "About a year and a half ago, this horse got an infection. No bite, no cuts, nothing; it just appeared out of nowhere." Telling the story now, BJ makes the aside, "Psychics love that, when it 'comes out of nowhere.'"

The horse's infection was bad enough "to where the vet said that the horse either had to be put down or operate on the leg. And even if you're not a horse person," BJ explains, "you have got to know that an animal that large is going to require some serious money to operate on a leg. Obviously they did that."

In an effort to make clear the connection to the owner, BJ asks, "Tell me about the little boy, then. What happened to him about a year and a half ago?"

A dog came out of nowhere, the owners explains, and bit the boy through to his leg, clear to his bone. It was a very severe bite. And they were about an hour from the hospital.

"Which leg was it?"

The left leg, the owner recalls. Infection and stitches were expected. The hospital was an hour away.

But, by the time they got to the hospital, the boy not only didn't need stitches, there wasn't even an infection.

"Do you get the connection here?" BJ asks.

The owner was floored. Then she began to remember other, seemingly insignificant details. "You know," she commented, "I've noticed that whenever we bring my son out here, he's never really cared for any of the horses we've had —he's just not a horse person, apparently—but he will run out here and hug this horse's legs."

Another moving story BJ recounts has to do with a similar gift of unconditional love on the part of pets.

An individual who was accompanying BJ and the horse owner during the incident just described commented on her own experience with these precious gifts.

"You know, BJ," the companion remarked, wide-eyed, "I have two cats who are deaf in the left ears, and my daughter is deaf in the right ear."

"Go home and kiss them," BJ advised seriously. "That's why your daughter can hear in the left ear."

BJ, author of the upcoming *For the Love of Animals, Our Other Guardian Angels,* has dozens of similar stories and more. The book will be available in your favorite bookstore late in 1999.

Directory of Intuitive Arts Practitioners

Following are names and phone numbers of Northwest practitioners of intuitive arts. Also included are practitioners who make regular visits to the Northwest and/or who will do phone readings for Northwest residents. (An asterisk (*) by the name indicates the practitioner has been visited by the author.)

All information included in this chapter is provided directly by the practitioner.

PLEASE NOTE: The information contained in this Directory is listed for information purposes only. The mission of this book is to present a platform of information from which an interested person may choose which practitioner to visit, if any. The author cannot guarantee that your visit to an intuitive arts practitioner will produce the results you desire. A listing in this book does not constitute an endorsement by the author, Trumpet Vine Press, its agents or assigns.

Alelyunas, Lino
Grass Valley, California
and Seattle, Washington
1-800-578-0781

*Clairvoyant • Trance-Channeler • Mystic Teacher •
Reiki Master • Certified Spiritual Healer • Minister •
Certified Meditation Instructor • Registered Counselor
• Tarot • Psychic Palmistry*

Lino is a born psychic discovered in 1981 by some
teachers at the Berkeley Psychic Institute after she had
some unexplainable mystical experiences.

She trained there for two years in an intensive
program on perceiving auras and chakras (energy centers in
the body). She also began to teach there, until her increasing
interest in mysticism led her to India on a spiritual path.
After studying with many spiritual Masters and living in
meditation ashrams, she was invited to teach at the Osho
Mystery School in Poona, India from 1987-1989 — a
school devoted to esoteric and spiritual knowledge. Here
she had the great fortune to meet, share and teach with some
of the most profound psychic healers, channelers and clairvoyants of our time.

She was invited to Australia to work out of The Center
of Balance in Perth, and then in 1991 came to Seattle to

open up her own Mystery School: Inner Light, which offers certification in Reiki, clairvoyance development and spiritual healing.

A session with Lino will reveal:

- Romance and relationship issues
- Career potentials
- Health concerns
- Past lives and karmic patterns
- Creative fulfillment
- Personality traits
- Family issues
- Messages and connection to your spirit guides
- Counseling and healing
- Spiritual guidance
- Future influences in all areas of life
- All questions answered.

(*) Allen, Madaline
West Linn, Oregon
(503) 636-8306

Psychic Consultant

Madaline Allen is a born psychic. Her gifts were apparent even as a small child growing up in San Francisco. She has been in private practice since 1983, and has developed into one of Oregon's top psychics. She is internationally known, with clients from all walks of life.

Madaline's goals for each client in personal consultations include:

- Helping and empowering people to work through their issues and problems.
- Teaching them how to set goals and achieve joy and fulfillment in life.
- Assisting them to develop their spiritual selves and to work with their Higher Power.
- Discovering their life's purpose and why they are here.
- Discussing with them their soul's journey in this lifetime.

An intuitive consultation with Madaline will bring you on a fascinating journey. Madaline begins by giving a basic lesson in which she teacher her method on how to "study and learn" yourself.

She will speak to you about centering the body, mind and spirit and how to change or improve the personal vibrations and energy around yourself.

She will talk to you about setting goals and using your innate power of mind and spirit to make things happen in your life as you wish them to.

She begins the reading by scanning you to check your health vibrations. She reads the Tarot and your numerology to see what number you were born under and what number you are presently in.

Madaline has a way of packaging everything for you in a very nice, neat package so that when you leave the consultation, you know exactly what you have to do to make your life better.

Give yourself or a friend a gift (gift certificates are available). It is a wonderful investment in yourself. Call for an appointment with Madaline, and let her take you on a unique and enlightening journey.

Ayo, Damali
(503) 230-9600
Portland, Oregon
www.tiac.net/users/rtoomey/ltyb

Healer • Psychic • Facilitator • Tarot

Inspiration. My true calling is to provide support to individuals, couples, and parents and children as they walk their life paths together and separately. I find the process of remembering our strengths and resources both beautiful and inspiring. Each of our paths takes twists and turns that teach us valuable lessons and provide opportunities for healing. We all benefit from having support as we navigate the lessons life holds for us. We often need help remembering our strengths, goals, and resources. Through a range of training and life experience, I have developed a system that helps people rediscover their ability to care for themselves and create reality of their dearest dreams. It is this eclectic system of support that I bring to our work together.

Insight. I have been developing my psychic gifts since I was a child. As a wise young girl I was aware of the spirits in my home and communicated with them often. I purchased and read my first Tarot cards at the age of 17 and have been doing readings ever since. I get a great deal of joy through accessing my psychic gifts to give insight and illumination to my clients. I use my own system of color reading, Tarot cards, as well as psychic gifts and guides to provide you with guidance as you navigate the tender curves of your life's path.

I am dedicated to the consistent expansion of my healing gifts and tools. I bring to our work the newest information from my healing and psychic guides. I use an ancient system of healing channeled from my ancestors that uses a wide range of tools and techniques to help your body, mind, and soul regenerate, cleanse and heal. This system helps you to feel activated and independent in your healing. I serve as a catalyst in your process and it is my goal to help you discover the tools you need to sustain your healing work independently.

Since 1990, I have been designing exercises and workshops that help people to regain connection with their inner selves. I have also pursued many areas in my own self-care and have brought these skills to my work. I utilize meditation practice and the power of movement. I design guided visualizations tailored to your needs and goals to help you reach parts of you buried deep inside. I have studied Eclectic Karate and enjoy bringing this beautiful and powerful martial art to my clients. I also use my skills as a writer and visual artist to support your expression of your inner self as you walk your life path.

I have developed a line of products to support and teach you as you grow and heal. I provide journals that offer you concrete exercises for regaining connection with yourself. I have a chakra guide that teaches you of the energy in and around your body. These and other unique tools help you on your path to deepen connection with yourself.

Working with me is a unique experience. I believe deeply in your own wisdom as I share my own. I delve deeply into your needs and the needs I perceive in your body and energy field. We work as partners in your healing and I serve as a companion for you as you walk delicate steps on your life path. Our goal is that you have your inner self as your constant companion, support, and guide throughout your entire life.

Commitment. I am wholly dedicated to seeing you rise like a phoenix and spread your beautiful bright wings for all to see. I hold full faith in your ability to heal and nurture yourself. I consider it an honor to be a witness and support at this moment in your life. The exercises and activities that I draw upon are wonderful resources and tools that you can use on your own. Finally, and most importantly, I dedicate my time with you to helping you remember how strong, beautiful, and capable you are. This work is about remembering what it is like to love yourself and communicate in a healthy way with all that is around you. It is an honor to be a piece of your process.

Bender, Connie
Eugene, Oregon
(541) 345-6235

Tarot • Intuitive Consulting • Astrology • Reiki • Classes

Connie Bender is an astrologer, Tarot reader, and psychic in Eugene, Oregon. She is an Oregon native who has studied mystical arts since she was 13. Connie does past-life regressions and counseling as well as individual natal and birthday readings. She is a Reiki Master and a registered minister who performs rituals and ceremonies for birthings, commitments, and transitions.

Connie is a regular reader at Eugene's Saturday Market and the Oregon Country Fair. Since 1988 she has helped clients with a variety of issues including personal process work, relationship problems, and career decisions. Her intuitive skills have been apparent since her childhood, when she learned dowsing from her grandfather. She is a beloved teacher of Tarot and astrology and an excellent public speaker on spiritual topics.

Connie has studied many spiritual traditions, from Native American to Buddhist. She is a descendent of the fairy people, and has particular empathy with etheric phenomena.

Connie has an ability to channel complex information in a manner that is useful to people who need to make decisions and who want to understand the passages on their journey. She has a deep visceral understanding of the importance of spirit in human development. Her readings for clients are grounded in compassion, love, and honesty.

Connie does consultations in person and by phone. She can be reached at the above number.

Bernadette
Seattle, Washington
(360) 675-8105

Psychic • Clairaudient • Psychometrist

Bernadette always wanted to know how and why things happened. Having had some psychic experiences, she began exploring different spiritual concepts. Starting with reincarnation, she began learning about healing and how important it is to heal the emotions and the mind as well as the body.

Clairaudient: Past Lives and Karma. As a psychic in a delta state, Bernadette receives audio phrases which augment her ability to counsel clients. Spiritual advisors help clarify situations perplexing to clients, giving them positive answers and helpful alternatives to any confusing situation, often enhancing spiritual growth. Many troubling predicaments that clients encounter are related to karmic obligations. Psychic readings often relieve trauma, clarifying and erasing problems associated with past incarnations.

Psychometry: As a psychometrist, Bernadette will ask to hold a personal object such as jewelry or even your hand to use as a conductor to receive your sensory radiations.

Dream Analysis: Dreams are symbolic of your subconscious trying to relate answers to everyday problems. Dreams are best interpreted by the dreamer who is often confused as to their meaning. A psychic can help delineate the meaning of symbols, thereby helping the dreamer understand their meaning.

Bernadette has attended many psychic fairs and is available for individual counseling.

(*) Berry
Portland, Oregon
(503) 727-2441
goldtiger@lycosemail.com

Upon the realization that our life has not worked out to our satisfaction, we oftentimes begin a search for greater self-fulfillment. Within the metaphysical/spiritual awareness community we find countless modalities from which to choose. Someone may choose only a single style, whereas another may be more eclectic and synthesize myriad methods to heal themselves and, in turn, others.

Throughout the past 25 years, Berry has explored and incorporated numerous healing tools and techniques into a working system. He instructs some of these modalities of healing to seekers for assistance in exploring their paths and in finding their own truths. Among these are meditation (yantra), aura healing, clairvoyant reading (all these first three part of raja yoga), rebirthing, Reiki, Freudian emotional work (sans hypnosis), men's issues group-work, inner-child group-work, and most recently, mahayana Buddhism in the Dzogchen lineage, studying Lama Surya Das.

Berry has facilitated classes and workshops aiding countless individuals in group settings as well as in private sessions. Locally, he has been on staff at a number of the finest healing centers.

(*) BJ
Animal Communications
Aloha, Oregon
(503) 848-9514
outside Oregon 1-800-730-7255

BJ has been dubbed the New Age Dr. Doolittle. She and her business, Animal Communications, have been featured on TV programs such as "The CBS This Morning Show" and the "Good Evening Show." She does radio talk shows all across the country and has had feature articles in *The Oregonian, The Seattle Times, The Boston Times* and in several magazines.

She not only talks to the animals, but also to the people who live with them, helping both to understand each other. She has been instrumental in helping people deal with the death of their pets and in finding those who are lost.

Her sessions are both insightful and fun and her upcoming book, *For the Love of Animals, Our Other Guardian Angels,* where she shares some of her funniest and most poignant animal stories, is sure to make the Best Seller's list.

"I have come to believe, in my years of helping people and their animals to communicate with each other, that our animal's souls are made up of a piece of our soul. In that, they can mirror us, can take on illnesses for us and they help us work on any issues that come up for us. They manifest our 'stuff' in the physical. I never know (oops, I guess that doesn't sound very psychic, does it? Well, my secret's out — I'm human just like all of you!) Anyway, I never know when that phone rings, what incredible story is going to unfold...Life just keeps getting more and more incredible, doesn't it?"

Boechler, Debbie
Aloha, Oregon
(503) 591-5230

Channeler • Reader

By simply allowing the light of unconditional love to fill my heart, I am able to provide useful, life-changing information to those individuals who wish to seek divine guidance. I hear direct communication from one's Higher Self, guides, angels, or deceased loved ones.

My goal in working with individuals, one-on-one, is to encourage a spiritual awakening, heal old emotional wounds, provide clear, concise messages that offer direction, as well as education about making direct communication with that individual's personal guides, teachers, or angels.

Receiving these divine messages and teachings from the universe enables individuals to make changes that are positively motivated in one's life.

I am available for individual or group readings.

Guided Group Meditation: Learning to meditate can be difficult. Come join in a guided group meditation, and share your experiences and/or frustrations.

The goal of the group is to use the collective energy of each individual within the group in order to experience the deep meditation and relaxation that is often difficult to achieve by one's self.

Each meditation is channeled from the guides, teachers, or angels for that specific group, giving each person exactly what they need at that particular time. These meditations may then be taken home and used on an individual basis.

A new meditation is presented each time the group meets and they vary from: self-healing techniques, emotional clearing of aura and bodies, earth-healing techniques, to resting within the light of the Christ consciousness and relaxation.

Not only is this group designed to teach the beginner, but the advanced as well, encouraging and assisting each individual to make contact with their own guides. Please call for class schedules. Evening and weekend times; drop-in structure; individual instruction available.

Boechler, Gary
Aloha, OR
(503) 591-5230

Healer • Energy Worker

By placing my hands on your shoulders, and working with our mutual guides, I move through your physical, spiritual, emotional, and mental bodies, clearing away any negative energies or blocks that are keeping you from healing. I see past-life issues that were unresolved and carried forward to now as well as emotional wounds from this life that are creating your particular physical or emotional illness.

I believe that the majority of all physical illnesses stem from emotional pain left unattended. By identifying these issues and removing any negative energy associated with them, it will enable you to begin your healing process.

Spirit only reveals what you are ready and able to work through at that particular time.

Please call for appointment times. Several sessions may be required.

Burke, H. Elizabeth, M.A.
Infinite Heart Insights
Portland, Oregon
(503) 256-4192

Psychic • Teacher • Channeler • Counselor-Therapist

Infinite Heart Insights is not a predictive work. A reading of this kind will not tell you where to go or what to do. It will, however, empower you to make clearer decisions and choices about the questions that arise in your life. It will give you things to think about and affirm intuitions you may already have.

A reading will also illuminate what is unknown, by working with your High Self and Source, and give you an opportunity to look at life's questions on an energetic level. From a reading, you will gain insights about hindrances that block your goals and process both at ordinary and spiritual levels. Fresh and innovative solutions and new perspectives that help you understand current problems and difficulties are often gained during a reading.

A reading will take you on a unique inner journey that clarifies your questions, illuminates your path and gives form and healing to your individual process. The motivation of this work is to provide you with guidance through the wisdom and compassion of Source and High Self; so you can make educated and informed choices that facilitate your own growth and healing.

The information obtained is known for its accuracy and practicality. Relationship and family issues, business and career strategies, life path, spiritual and psychological growth and questions about past lives are a few areas that can be explored.

Elizabeth's readings combine deep compassionate wisdom, empathic and psi insights with grounded counseling techniques to provide a heartfelt and enlightening experience for each client. Elizabeth has done this work and been a counselor, and conscious channel since 1985. She has taught around the country and throughout the Southwest for the past 10 years and is honored to be serving the NW community. She available by phone or in person.

Classes and Trainings: (The Inward Journey - Awakening the World Within; a three-part chakra, intuition, and wisdom training)

E'ala is the first course in The Inward Journey training. During E'ala students will be introduced to their inner world. Each chakra will be awakened in a gentle and effective manner. Each person will learn to read the energy and the patterns within the chakras and being. A basic understanding of where blocks are held and why they exist is another benefit gained during this course. Students will learn ways to maintain grounding to stay centered even in the most chaotic times, and learn clearing and protection techniques as well. Wisdom teachings from Buddhist, Taoist and Hawaiian shamanic traditions and Western psychic traditions will also be taught.

In part two, Ho'okino, students will learn how to move fluidly across time and space delving into the body and the "body of knowledge." This work is an original process and is a part of a deeper work called the Integrated

Embodiment Process™. Each person will begin to understand why they habitually behave or respond to problems
and challenges the way they do. They will learn to
transform old patterns, and integrate new ways of being,
releasing their own suffering in the process. Students will
explore deeply their cellular body.

The last course, Malamalama, returns to the chakras
and energy system where each chakra is revisited and
through the use of sound and vibration further awakened.
New material often surfaces as students delve more deeply
into the nature of their individual embodied experience. An
understanding of one's life purpose and the purpose of this
incarnation are explored. Further study of the obstacles and
the mystery of embodiment are also examined.

Elizabeth also teaches Hawaiian shamanic and meditation techniques as well as the Integrated Embodiment
Process ™ to other therapists, individuals and couples.

Classes are taught throughout the year, with beginning
classes in the Inward Journey training forming in the fall,
winter and spring. Call for details and schedules about this
training and other day-long workshops.

Therapy: Integrated Embodiment Process ™

Our chakras, energy system and body are conscious
and deeply alive. If we wish to, we can access the entire
history of our being through the body, and chakras. By
gaining access to this body of knowledge we can answer
our most perplexing questions.

During the Integrated Embodiment Process ™ (IEP) I
create and hold a vast space so you can explore your inner
world — safely and deeply. By working with me you also
come to know the heart of your being that is connected to
your high Self and Source. You learn to see your patterns as
they are embodied and learn ways to transform them at your

core. I have traveled into the core of my being to heal myself, so I know the way.

For over 20 years I have studied the nature of mind and its relationship to healing. I have trained with Taoist priests, Buddhist monks, Hawaiian shamans and Western healers and hold a Master's Degree in contemplative and somatic psychology and counseling. I forged the Integrated Embodiment Process from this experience; combining it with that of meditation, tempering it with the wisdom, humor and compassion from Buddhist and Taoist traditions, and wedding it finally to psychology.

IEP is valuable in dealing with spiritual and life transitions, relationship issues, loss and grief, childhood trauma, physical and psychosomatic symptoms and repetitive patterns of behavior and thinking that limit the individual. Past-life experiences can also be integrated and understood by using the Integrated Embodiment Process. The confusion that occurs during spiritual emergence phenomena and transpersonal states can also be helped with IEP.

In 1990, I created the Integrated Embodiment Process; since then I have developed IEP and written a book on this new therapy.

Byrnes, Diane, LMT
Spirit Wind Communications
Portland, Oregon
(503) 224-2145

Intuitive • Healer • Channeler

I have been practicing healing and bodywork for the past 20 years. Though I have always been intuitive and clairaudient, it has been since 1997 that my work has evolved to include vibrational healing, chakra balancing and channeled spirit guided readings.

For the duration of my career as a massage therapist, I have received images and messages about my clients which helped to deepen their healing process and expand their awareness of what was occurring in their lives on all levels: body, mind, and spirit.

Currently my work has reached a new level and is primarily about assisting people to release unserving patterns held in the etheric body, and to help them connect directly with their own intuition and spirit guides. Using sound (crystal bowls, voice toning, drumming, rattle and bells), crystals, energy work and vibrational healing essences, this work creates an alchemical healing that often produces dramatic and transformative results for the client.

I always work with a number of Masters, guides and angels, including the angel Metatron and St. Germain of the Violet Flame.

Also I do readings, answer questions and give assistance in contacting your personal guides and angels. The intention I hold for all sessions is to empower the client to absolutely know he or she has the ability to access the truth within, and receive the guidance requested.

My guides have been telling me it's time to come forward, speak up, and share this work with others. In this time of accelerated growth, change and spiritual awakening, the most important message my guides have given to me and my clients is "Ask for help and remember you are not alone. Allow your guides to come forward to assist you in your life. The time is now. Open your heart to yourself and others. We are all one."

Caldwell, Diane, LMT
Clackamas, Oregon
(503) 698-3072
dcaldwell@imagina.com

Clairvoyant • Healer

Life presents us with many opportunities for growth. The path through these challenging life events can often be unclear. As a clairvoyant I help a person reach the information about their life that may not be available to them. I then assist the person in gaining clarity, understanding, and a fresh perspective around their issues.

I have several techniques that I use in my readings, including Rose, Chakra, Past Life and Soul Essence. I use these techniques to access knowledge that brings into focus a picture of where a person is now on their personal journey, enabling them to make informed decisions about their life path. I work with people on issues relating to all areas of life including personal growth, spiritual evolution, health, home, work, and relationships, including other people and animals.

In times of transformation our bodies also need support. In addition to working as a clairvoyant, I also work as a healer. I have a deep understanding of people and their bodies as a result of ten years of experience as a Licensed Massage Therapist and my own process of healing the body/mind connection. I can assist a person by working with universal energy to clear out physical and emotional blocks, and to open pathways for healing and diving energies to fully flow.

Since my graduation from the Earth School Institute three years ago and becoming a professional clairvoyant, I have been assisting people in the journey of becoming more fully who they are.

Please contact me for more information about my work as a clairvoyant, and how I can be of service to you.

Campbell, Ed
Seattle, Washington
(206) 783-3410
<http://www.edcampbell.com>

Palmistry • Author • Teacher • Lecturer

I have been practicing hand analysis for many years, and teaching it since 1986. In 1996 my book, *The Encyclopedia of Palmistry,* was published by the Perigee division of the Berkley-Putnam publishing group. It has received excellent reviews both in the United States and in the United Kingdom and is rated one of the best, most thorough books on the subject available. Most recently I have helped found the Northwest Hand Institute for the scientific study of the hand in relation to character and health. I am also a consultant to an international study on the feasibility of using the fingerprints and other ridge and line patterns of the palm as diagnostic markers for disease.

I enjoy traveling. This allows me to observe people who chose to live in different parts of the world and the differences that show up on their hands. For example, there appear to be significant differences in the general shape of the hands of those who prefer living in the desert Southwest United States as compared to those who would rather live on the Pacific Coast. I have lectured and participated in major shows on both coasts, in New York, Atlanta and Tampa on the East Coast, and Portland, Seattle and Vancouver, British Columbia on the West Coast, as well as shown in Calgary and Edmonton in Canada. In the southwest and west, visits have included lectures and shows in Phoenix, Tucson, Las Vegas, Reno and Salt Lake City. Many communities with smaller populations have also been visited, especially throughout Washington and Oregon. My home is in Seattle.

The background to my intuitive skills is varied. I have been in the private practice of law since 1966. As a boy I played in haunted houses, bombed-out buildings and abandoned mansions in England, and the woods of the Southeastern and Midwestern United States. I am trained in alternative forms of health care, being a Licensed Massage Practitioner and a Guild Certified Feldenkrais Practitioner®. I helped found the International Assembly of Spiritual Healers & Earth Stewards Congregations in 1988, and that organization can now count among its several thousands of ordained participants, ministers from every continent except Antarctica. As a weekly talk show radio host I frequently have psychics as guests, along with others from the world of science, health care, law, religion, ecology, labor, industry and finance. At this time my show is heard on stations WALE AM in Providence, Rhode Island, and KFNX AM in Phoenix, Arizona on early Wednesday evenings.

While having studied such other arts and crafts as iridology, use of herbs, astrology, Tarot, numerology, past life regression, and even having practiced a little exorcism, I choose to use my intuitive skills in conjunction with my hand analysis. I am available by appointment for private consultations, and by arrangement for guest appearances, lectures, events and expositions. For more information you may visit my web site at the location listed above.

Childs, Ruth
Portland, Oregon
(503) 775-9225

Aura Photography • Aura Readings • Energy Readings • Energy Healings • Hypnotherapy • Regressions • Psychic Healer • Psychic Counselor • Chakra Alignment • Healing • Teacher • Lecturer

I have been working with aura photography for 15 years up and down the West Coast and throughout Canada with appearances at various psychic fairs and expos. I am still frequently to be found at psychic fairs/expos and I am also promoting some new fairs and occasionally appear at bookstores and clinics with the aura camera. I would be delighted to use the aura camera as a fundraiser for your organization.

I've seen auras all my life and have been giving aura and energy readings for over 30 years; helping people experience more peace, love and joy; giving confirmation, and sometimes bringing closure to an issue. A typical reading is approximately 50 minutes in length and is taped. Clients often leave feeling serene, confident, assured and positive-minded. Many lives have been healed and turned around as a result of hearing the right words at the right time.

My hypnosis training in Alchemical and Transformative Hypnotherapy was completed in 1992 at East-West College in Portland, Oregon. I specialize in regressions, addictions, and clearing negative programming. I trained under Rosalyn Bruyere with chakra alignment and healing energy of the body. I've also studied some with Donna Evans in body electro-magnetic energy fields and kinesiology.

Occasionally, I teach workshops dealing with auras, colors, symbols, and also assist participants in developing their own intuitive gifts. I am available for private groups and churches if they wish to sponsor a class. I teach energy chelation and healing also.

I would be happy to assist you in any challenge you are currently facing. Call me at the above number in Portland, Oregon.

Christianson, Vivian
(see Vivian)

Christopher, Darleen
Edmonds, Washington
(425) 640-9759

*Astrology • Teacher • Medical Intuitive • Numerology
• Palm Reading • Tarot • (Also speaks American Sign
Language)*

As an empathic clairvoyant counselor, practiced
palmist and Tarot reader, I am able to assist in unleashing
the barriers in one's life. I study astrology and numerology.
I invoke prayer, hear the client's name and receive information.

By focusing on past, present, and future influences,
we can explore a revitalized, clearer, empowered direction.
Open up your physical, mental, and spiritual world to inner
peace.

Palm and fingerprint patterns have been found
throughout the world at ancient excavation sites. Aristotle
looked into the hands for revealing health. Hippocrates
discovered a correlation between the hand and the condition
of the lungs. By utilizing palmistry, one can have clues
where health, talents, career, emotional bondage, spiritual
and matters of the heart are concerned. So much energy
comes from our hands. Palmistry is an empowering tool.

Our brain sends impulses out to the tips of the fingers where knowledge is recorded. "God seals up the hand of every man, that all men may know their work" (Job 37:7).

In a Tarot reading, we will explore with the synergistic assistance of your subconscious mind and our guides working together to promote inner harmony and balance.

I have been practicing palmistry and Tarot since 1992, and have studied esoteric knowledge since childhood. I have appeared at numerous psychic fairs and parties. I'm a published writer, study metaphysics, psychology, English literature, film and liberal arts.

Available for private or phone consultation and parties by appointment or at participating psychic fairs.

(*) Clarkson, Don
Portland, Oregon
(503) 295-9777
Toll-Free 1-888-474-9153
e-mail: espman2@aol.com

Psychic • Tarot • Personal Coaching

Don is a full-time psychic with 18 years experience meeting the needs of local, national and international clients through his office in Portland, his home overlooking the Columbia River Gorge, and through telephone and Internet readings. A left-brain Virgo and born-again skeptic, Don welcomes your skepticism or hesitation and is happy to discuss your concerns or send brochures and newsletters before you commit to an appointment. Credit cards or payment arrangements are gladly accepted.

A typical day's clients included an attorney with questions on a case; a man troubled by his alcoholism; a woman "stuck" in her career; two clients with undiagnosed illnesses. Of course, all were looking for love, too!

Typically, clients express the concerns or areas of interest, and then Don closes his eyes for a few minutes, goes into his mental "Workshop" and watches pictures form. He takes a few notes and then goes over the notes in a normal conversation with the client, avoiding any "weirdness" or high drama. He makes sure to cover all the client's questions, but often the "Workshop" has a mind of its own and will bring up issues of importance the client may not yet be aware of, such as health problems.

Don also uses Tarot cards as an adjunct to the reading. He has studied through the B.O.T.A. association for nearly 17 years and considers the ancient Tarot the foundation of his spiritual belief system, and finds it a profound way to access a client's subconscious and suggest future events and actions.

The best reading is when a client leaves the office saying "You didn't tell me anything I didn't already know, on some level." The work then is to integrate the information and the impact of a reading into the client's life. For this reason, Don does a large part of his work on the telephone with short, follow up sessions to help keep a client utilizing the psychic information.

He has also instituted a new program of Personal Coaching to formalize this process into weekly meetings with a client for goal setting and progress reporting. Hearing information through the psychic process is one thing, but fully using it to make growth changes in life is quite another, and with this added service of Coaching, Don is able to impact a client's life in an on-going fashion. Don's psychic clients are fully able to use his Coaching services, and his Coaching clients make full use of his psychic abilities.

Anyone interested in more information about Don's readings, classes, or Personal Coaching services are encouraged to call for a discussion with Don, or ask for a free brochure.

Readings: In Portland, Oregon at 1020 SW Taylor, Suite 205, Portland 97205. Also in the Columbia River Gorge, if you are looking for a short daytrip with breathtaking views. Telephone, E-mail, and Internet readings are increasingly popular with busy clients — no driving, no parking, just quick information. Call for rates and payment options. Money should never be an obstacle to a reading.

Classes: Don has taught an intensive Tarot class for four years, using the Tarot as a springboard to personal growth. This is not a "how to read" the cards class, but rather "how are you living" the cards? Students may join at any time.

Don teaches a popular class on how to visualize and manifest your desires into concrete form. Classes are offered every two months. Call for dates.

Mystical Merriment: Don has a "stable" of metaphysical practitioners, such as psychics, astrologers, Tarot readers, an animal psychic, and others to entertain and enlighten your next business meeting, holiday party, or social gathering of whatever nature. Call for rates and brochure.

Coaching. Having a Personal Coach "on your side," interested in your welfare, aware of your needs and wants, can be the difference between Hoping and Becoming. Don can be a kind and gentle listener and then he can become a gentle prod, that extra push that helps you become who you want to be. Call for more information on the benefits of having a Personal Coach.

Clouden, Lori (Rev.)
Lakewood, Colorado
(303) 988-3950

Psychic • Healer • Teacher

Hello! I am Rev. Lori Clouden. I'm a clairvoyant reader, healer, and teacher and Director of the Inner Connection Institute of Metaphysics (ICIM). I'm also a minister with the Church of Inner Light of Boulder, Colorado. I offer clairvoyant readings, energetic healings, psychic development training, breathwork, ceremonies and counseling.

Like many psychics, I have been sensitive to the energy of people and places since childhood. As a child and young adult, my sensitivity created many challenges for me until I began to consciously work with energy. My conscious spiritual journey began with seven years of personal and spiritual cleansing. I then completed formal clairvoyant training through two prominent psychic institutes in Portland, Oregon and Denver, Colorado. I completed ministry training through the Church of Inner Light. I am committed to continuing my self-discovery and hope that my own personal growth keeps my work fresh and evolving. In my practice, I hope to support others in discovering and expressing their own unique essence, talents, and spiritual power.

Clairvoyant readings are the basis of my work and one of my most requested services. A reading is a great way to get a fresh perspective on challenges, opportunities, and relationships. When I read, I begin with a prayer to set the energy. Readings have no set structure. The format is unique for each individual, according to his or her needs. Generally, a reading is driven by questions or issues about which the client would like greater clarity. Information comes through a variety of avenues, including input I receive by clairvoyantly viewing the spiritual body and aura, communication from my spiritual helpers, and messages from the client's own spirit guides and soul essence.

Readings usually uncover what's blocking the client from creating what he/she desires in his/her life. Unconscious patterns, belief systems and outside influences from others are brought to light, and one can see clearly his or her own path. Readings may be conducted in person or over the telephone. Audiotapes are provided.

I conduct healings with the assistance of loving, powerful healing guides, whom I know well and trust impeccably. I channel these guides through my hand chakras to work with the client's energy. Healings help open, balance and re-align the chakras, cleanse the body's energy pathways, and cleanse the aura. A number of techniques may be employed, depending upon the individual's needs. Healings facilitate the release of blockages to growth and toxic energies, and restore the free flow of life force energy. Healings are a great tool for moving through times of difficult transition, health challenges or "feeling stuck." Often, readings and healings are conducted at the same time to first identify challenges and then shift the blocked energy creating the problem.

Readings and/or healings may be performed for individuals, couples, groups, and even on homes and businesses. For more information about readings, healings, classes, or the other services I offer, please give me a call at the number above. A free newsletter is also available, so please feel free to call if you'd like a copy.

Cole, Dorothy M.Ed.
Healing for All
Hood River, Oregon
(503) 524-1822
Heal4All@aol.com

Spiritual Healer • Shaman

Personal History. In 1993, Dorothy Ann was injured in a car accident, experiencing a closed head injury which blocked her ability to think for nearly two years. Her ability to think with her left brain impaired, Dorothy Ann learned to think differently with her right brain, becoming more intuitive and aware. This episode in her life forced her to change her world view, moving from being an agnostic scientist to a spiritual teacher and healer. Taking this quantum leap, Dorothy Ann emerged as a spiritual healer, working holistically with the mind, body and spirit of her clients. One day, God gave Dorothy Ann a gift which showed before-and-after photographic evidence that her spiritual practices affect blood cells, using dark field blood samples. The article with pictures is available upon request.

Background. Dorothy Ann Cole, M.Ed., began her career teaching high school science, later teaching psychology and philosophy at the university level in Alaska. She earned a B.S. cum laude from UC Berkeley in Conservation of Natural Resources, a B.A. in Language and

Cognition from The Evergreen State College, won a Rotary Foundation Graduate Fellowship and studied at the University of Sheffield in England, earning her Masters in Education. She completed half the doctorate program at the University of San Francisco in Curriculum and Instruction and holds an Honorary Doctorate of Divinity. Dorothy Ann has always been an educator, entrepreneur, and explorer of new thought, bridging science and spirituality.

Auraopathy. Clearing auras is Dorothy Ann's specialty. She rids people of discarnate energies which impede people from reaching their true potential. Clearing the aura is a purification process which allows people to know "who they really are." According to Donald Neale Walsch, *Conversations With God,* knowing who we really are is our soul purpose. Auraopathy, the pathology of the aura, allows people to begin their spiritual journey free of negative encumbrances. These subtle releases transform people who release intense negative emotion, negative self-talk, and sometimes disease or health problems including depression, manic depression, diabetes, prostate problems, and schizophrenia. (See the article entitled, "Auraopathy: the New Medicine" located on the Internet at the following: http://www.castle.net/~mystic/pages/spirheal.html. Be sure to scroll down for the title page.)

Noetic Medicine. In 1998, Dorothy Ann discovered that what she has been guided to do is the work of a shaman, including exorcising spirits; releasing hexes, curses, and spells, and disempowering dark force energies. Dorothy Ann realized her research was evolving into Noetic Medicine, comprised of advanced clearing activities in 13 bodies or energy fields. Noetic Medicine means energy work beyond the five senses and third dimensional reality. Noetic Medicine goes beyond the five senses into multi-

dimensions, clearing disease energies or negative thinking
or irrational emotionalism from the following: past, present,
future, and parallel lives, parallel universe, alternate
realities, and current life. The present life is the current
moment, and the current life is the life in this time and space
on the earth plane.

Hands-on and TRIOM. Another day, Dorothy Ann had
her chakras opened by a Vietnamese woman who
announced afterward, "You now have hands-on healing gift.
You practice. Move hands close together and back. You see
smoke!" Dorothy Ann later realized that she meant energy.
The source of the gift is a Vietnamese Buddhist monk
named Desire' Narada who passed over in 1924. Always
Dorothy Ann seeks spiritual practices that people can do for
themselves and found a procedure known as TRIOM. This
extraordinarily simple technique allows lay people to do
skin-to-skin touching work and produce powerful results in
areas of cancer, migraines, epilepsy, Chronic Fatigue
Syndrome, lupus, fibromyalgia, Attention Deficit
Hyperactivity Disorder (ADHD), and AIDS. One AIDS
client had a viral load drop from 300,000 to 25 a few
months after the AIDS procedure and feels great.

Education and Philosophy. Dorothy Ann believes that
healing comes from within a person who truly desires to
heal. Most of the practices she uses, she teaches to her individual clients and to other healers to empower themselves.
Current courses include Auraopathy: A New Medicine;
AKABA: A Transformational Healing Practice; Spiritual
Response Therapy; Noetic Medicine; and TRIOM. She also
offers this information in workshops and seminar formats
and is available to do public speaking for conferences or
interested groups. Dorothy Ann writes a column, "On the
Spiritual Edge" for *Community ConneXions,* hosts a cable

television show, "The Spiritual Edge," and is the founder of A Holistic Health Association (AHHA) in Portland, Oregon. Dorothy Ann Cole operates her practice in White Salmon, Washington, and provides consultations over the phone. Her client base extends to over 30 states and Canada.

Cornell, Karen
Angelwood Center
Seattle, Washington
(206) 729-2320
(800) 421-1682
www.angelwood.com

During the past 35 years, while raising six children, Karen found herself drawn to the world of metaphysics and the developing of her own psychic abilities. During the 70's she took a course in numerology. Being a math person, she was fascinated with what the numbers could tell her about herself as well as others. Twenty years later, she still enjoys the uniqueness of every chart!

Several years ago, Karen began doing readings using a conventional deck of cards. The cards and numerology work well together, as numerology tells things in larger blocks of time, and the cards bring the focus into what is happening right now and for the next few months. The combination gives a more complete picture of current events and brings answers to her clients with amazing clarity and accuracy.

In recent years, Karen participated as a reader in Boeing Parapsychology Club Fairs, Body Mind and Spirit Expo's, and has made numerous appearances at The Psychic Showcase as both guest speaker and reader. She has worked with Northwest psychics William Rainen, Shirlee

Teabo, Doug Johnston and Shirley Witt. She has been featured as the guest numerologist in "The Curious Psychic" column in the *Tacoma News Tribune*. For several years Karen has been a regular on local radio stations taking calls, discussing numerology and psychic abilities. Currently she is also the hostess on the "Psychic Northwest and Beyond" television show. You may also find her doing "mini-readings" in local restaurants and nightclubs. Residing in Seattle, Karen recently opened the Angelwood Center with her partner Liz MacDonald where they both do private readings and conduct classes and workshops.

Workshops: Workshops are conducted in Beginning and Advanced Numerology, Conventional Card Reading, Spiritual Growth, Color and Foods for Life.

Parties: Karen is available for private parties of all kinds. We also have a "party plan" for the ambitious hostess who would like to have two psychics, Karen and Liz, at her event, please call for details.

Weddings: If you are planning a wedding, Karen is a minister of the Universal Life Church and is available for your special occasion. Ceremony planning and counseling included in this service.

Dalton-Kash, Bethany
Oakland, California
(510) 339-0815

Shaman • Teacher

Bethany has been teaching urban shamanism skills in the San Francisco Bay Area since 1989. Her work is a compilation of ancient cross-cultural practices and modern-day spiritual and meditative disciplines.

She is the founder of an Oakland school which has taught numerous students to become professional psychics and healers.

A large portion of her work has been devoted to helping people in the creative arts, such as dancers, musicians, artists, and people in the film industry, bring psychic and spiritual skills into their work. Students are accepted internationally, but must show a certain level of competence to complete the program and dedicate themselves to the classwork, as it is advanced level training. Working with Bethany is more than a workshop or classes, it is a lifestyle change, where the students will awaken their deepest levels of knowing.

De Coriolis, Janet
Bellevue, Washington
(425) 881-8481 or
Stargazers (425) 885-7289

Psychic • Teacher • Reiki

Since 1974 I have been actively involved with the awakening of consciousness for myself and others. My journey has included meditation and study with various teachers of healing, channeling, psycho-social development and energetic transformation.

Over the last eight years, I have devoted time to the study and practice of two methods of touch therapy called Light Touch and Reiki. Three years ago I became a Reiki Master and currently offer private Reiki sessions, teach Reiki classes and hold a monthly Reiki Circle for those who want to practice and develop their healing skills. Reiki is a wonderful gift for anyone who is interested in personal growth and self-healing or foresees a time when they would like to facilitate others as they move through their process of awakening.

In 1993 I was awakened as a channel for Christ Consciousness (unconditional love). Working in partnership with Sananda, I offer private counseling sessions, regular channeled classes and support groups that encourage self-empowerment and awakening to the Spirit within.

I have had several articles published in the *New Times* and have written a book to accompany an as-yet unpublished deck of Tarot cards called the *Tarot of Awakening*.

The most important truth I have learned is that life is a process of unfolding and awakening to our true nature. This means that every minute of our day supports us as we learn about ourselves and our connection with the creative source from which we have emerged. Walking the spiritual path requires us to take some time each day to experience the sacredness of life. Simple practices such as meditation and prayer support our ability to stay conscious, but taking time daily to review our actions so that we can see where we might have behaved in a more loving manner is also important. In this way we learn to live consciously and take responsibility for ourselves and our actions. There are initiations and teachers that can help us to open to more dimensions of our being, but as individuals we choose how to integrate and manifest what we have been shown. Learning to honor the Christ within helps us to flourish and develop a relationship with the Creator that is unique and personal.

Devereux, Carole
Banks, Oregon
(503) 628-8403
e-mail: devereux@teleport.com
web page:
http://www.teleport.com/~devereux

***Animal Communications • Astrology • Spiritual
Growth Counselor • Writer***

As a writer, animal communicator, astrologer and spiritual growth counselor, I am able to use my skills in telepathic communication with my horses to help raise consciousness regarding the humane treatment of animals. After six years of study and training with the world's leading communicators, Dr. Jeri Ryan, psychologist, animal communicator and TTouchTM Practitioner, and author, poetess and sociologist Penelope Smith, I am writing a book about interspecies communication (with my horses, Buddy and Ellie). This book talks about equine spirituality and the evolution of the horse, focusing on the cyclical interrelation between humans and horses, beginning in the last Ice Age and continuing into the present day. I show how primal, early human communication with animals has contributed to modern-day spirituality, beginning with animism, totemism, shamanism and paganism.

In September, 1995, I traveled to the south of France to study the cave paintings. As a result, I gained a broader perspective of ancient animal communication and shamanism and how each one relates to our current revival of these "lost arts." Using journeying, meditation, music, dance, intuition, and spiritual guidance, I reveal how reverence towards ancient wild horses and other animals has elevated the human spirit throughout the ages, and continues to do so. My book merges current metaphysical philosophies with discussions on how to meditate with animals to achieve peace in your home, love in your heart and joyful relations among all species on earth and beyond. My book *Spirit of the Horse* will be in bookstores in 1999.

Once a year, I sponsor Dr. Jeri Ryan's Animal Communication Workshop and work with her to promote her newly founded Assisi International Animal Institute. Currently, I serve on the advisory board of the Institute, located in Monterey, California. I also conduct practice group sessions and basic and advanced workshops. I produced an introductory lecture on audio tape with Dr. Ryan, and have my own video on basic animal communication, as well as a quarterly Journal.

I am qualified to teach Penelope Smith's Basic Animal Communication Workshop, (the result of her 15 years of experience teaching interspecies telepathy across the U.S.). I have also developed seven spiritual meditations of my own, designed to grow human potential for working with interspecies communications to renew connections to our Source.

For more information about workshops, lectures, or private consultations, please contact me through the numbers listed above.

Dianna, Lisa
The Energy Within
Portland, Oregon
(503) 761-2080

Sensitive • Intuitive • Empath

Lisa specializes in energy. She uses her five senses in their heightened state as well as her sixth sense to explore the seen and unseen realms of existence.

Using this "second sight" with her clients has been very rewarding and extremely profound. With the intention of healing, Lisa Dianna invites into each and every session the highest form of light/energy. This merges with her assurance that the work is always done in purity, with love and integrity. Only that which is of the best and highest good for all shall enter and be brought forth in this energy work.

Lisa Dianna has always been incredibly sensitive. This was her way of interacting in this world since her birth. At times it did seem to be a heavy burden to have her five senses receiving information that others apparently were not also receiving. Experiencing life from that place was confusing, frustrating, isolating and sometimes hurtful. But with the blessings of family members and friends who understood her and loved her, these gifts were enhanced rather than shamed and buried. She feels joy and peace at this time in her life in bringing forward these gifts for the benefit of all.

With these gifts, Lisa Dianna receives information in different ways for different people. All are given as clues, in a symbolic language pointing us in the right direction for the work that is ready to be done at this time.

No two sessions are the same. It is difficult to describe what one might expect from an energy session. Every person is unique and so each person's session will be different, depending upon which avenue you choose.

Some work can be done using the mental body's verbal skills. Other sessions may focus on the body with touch and can be physical in nature. Another therapeutic technique involves brushing/combing the aura, the invisible and very real electromagnetic field that surrounds your body. The work on the auric field can be done without any hands-on touching. There are many other forms that invite the energy to return to its natural, balanced state where it can flow freely.

There are a variety of approaches to consider. Lisa Dianna will make suggestions on which modality of healing may best suit you and your specific circumstances. It is co-creative in nature, which means you are a key element in the choice process of your healing journey.

Trust yourself to know what your next step is. Listen to your inner voice and it will take you on to the next level of your healing journey.

(*) Dodich, Mark F.
Astromark
Portland, Oregon
(503) 252-1558
e-mail: mardo@europa.com
www.europa.com/~mardo/
astromark.html

***Astrology • Intuitive Tarot • Moses Numerology •
Animal Medicine Wheel Readings***

I have been serving people who are interested in soul growth since 1980. In addition to working with current and incoming life cycles, I feel it is important to understand the higher meaning of the events you attract into your life. Taking this extra step empowers you to make wise and loving choices for the highest good.

Astrology: The Initial Astrology Reading is the best place to start. We look at your talents, challenges, and incoming cycles of opportunity. My second-most popular reading is Earthlines. This geographical reading (aka Astrocartography® maps your personal power zones for travel, relocation, and business expansion.

For people focused upon soul purpose, Soul Ray Esoteric Astrology Readings are an excellent follow up to your Initial Astrology Reading. Based upon Alice Bailey's channelings of Djwahl Kuhl and the ancient mystery schools, you receive information on the Universal seven rays as it pertains to your life path. This helps you to call in a greater expression of your Divine Nature for increased soul service.

Relationship Astrology helps improve understanding and purpose in romance, family, and business partnerships.

Business Astrology helps you maximize opportunities for success by helping you to choose new employees, incorporation dates, produce introduction times, and a great deal more.

Group Dynamic Astrology improves communication, cooperation, and productivity for executive project teams, families, and sports teams.

Intuitive Spiritual Counseling: Intuition and Tarot are used to help you understand the changing energies in your life. We transcend amazing predictions like those offered on "900" psychic hotlines in favor of deep level understanding of the issues and opportunities you are manifesting in your life. This helps you to increase the quality of your life. Animal Medicine Wheel Readings taps into the understanding that all things are interconnected. Animals bring messages and power to help you walk in harmony with Great Spirit.

Moses Numerology: Based upon Cabalistic teachings and the Hebrew alphabet, this esoteric form of numerology helps you understand your physical and spiritual karma, talents, goals, and soul destiny in this incarnation. This unique method of numerology helps you to activate your soul purpose.

Background: Mark Dodich has been providing spiritual astrology and intuitive readings since 1980. He has served as president of the Oregon Astrological Association, and as a board member on other metaphysical organizations. Mark provides workshops and consultations interna-

tionally. His training includes the ministry program through the Church of Tzaddi and the Arizona Metaphysical Society. Mark's main love is helping people to access and increase the activation of their soul purpose. He can be reached at (503) 252-1558, mardo@eruopa.com, or visit his monthly astrology update at
www.europa.com\~mardo/astromark.html

Elizabeth, Quin
Portland, Oregon
(503) 231-5427

Shaman Journeys* • *Intuition Reclaiming* • *Guided Imagery* • *I Ching Readings

Quin is a contemporary shaman and spiritual guide. Her experience of spiritually awakening and traveling on a path of shamanic initiation makes her uniquely equipped to assist you on your path, wherever you are. With loving presence, compassion and clarity, Quin may use an oracle reading, guided imagery or shamanic counsel to help you learn to navigate through blocks and patterns that hinder your connection with your inner guidance. As you gain emotional clarity, you gain confidence in your innate connection to the universe through your intuition and realize that you have all the answers within you, you may just need a guide to help you find them.

Classes and individual mentoring available.

Engles-Smith, Jan
LightSong Healing Center
Gresham, Oregon
(503) 669-3013

Shaman • Reiki • Counseling • Author

Connection to spirit and the spiritual realm is your birthright; it does not come from someone else. Loving Spirit and desiring a relationship with Spirit helps our connection grow and develop. I believe there are many ways to reach Spirit, and exploring different methods leads to the enfoldment of the soul. In my practice I facilitate a person on their personal journey of bringing Spirit into their life and learning how to care for their own soul. Our indigenous forefathers understood the care of the soul to be the most important aspect of human life; few people understand this today.

Life is the journey of becoming. The more you become, the more you can become in a continual cycle of evolving. At what rate you choose to evolve will depend on you. The spiritual path is a choice that offers phenomenal rewards and is a totally personal experience.

Jan Engels-Smith is the author of *Becoming Yourself: The Journey from Head to Heart*. In this book Jan presents concepts and universal truths about healing and working with energy. This information stems from her own personal experiences, experiences of her clients and from the direct teaching from her spirit guides. The book reaches the heart of individual readers and encourages and motivates them to develop their own connection into the spirit realm. This book was generated from Jan's client base requesting that she print the amazing teaching that she has received.

To receive a copy of this book please contact the author.

Jan is available by appointment for:
• Personal Soul Retrievals
• Extraction and Healing work
• Chakra balancing and opening energy channels
• Reiki cleansing
• Shamanic crystal removal
• Shamanic counseling
• Traditional Counseling
• EMDR - Rapid Eye Movement Therapy
• Hypnotherapy
• Hypnosis
• Marriage and Family Counseling
• Guided Imagery tapes for healing: Jan will provide
 you with your personal tape custom-designed for
 your own particular needs.

For a calendar of workshops, drumming circles, retreats, and teaching circles, please contact Jan directly.

Fontaine, Marie
Portland, Oregon
(503) 977-9499

Visionary Artist • Healer • Teacher

Marie Fontaine is a visionary artist, author and teacher of meditation and healing. Sharing her inner vision through her work, she is dedicated to the expansion of personal awareness. Marie has traveled all over the world, exploring many cultures and spiritual traditions, finding a rich diversity and many commonalities in their forms of meditation and healing. She has studied with masters of yogic meditation, Dzogchen Tibetan Buddhism, Western metaphysical healing, Reiki, Egyptian Huna and Native American shamanic practices. A deep love and respect for the spiritual pathways of all people is the basis through which her work is given, acknowledging them as the "many manifestations of the One."

"My joy is to share the experiences found in meditation through a variety of forms. Each tradition has a slightly different energy texture or color. Some people are more in tune with one or another of these differences and will be drawn to a different tradition — it seems to work according to their own makeup and needs. I like to come from a

'universal perspective' while focusing on a 'specific branch
of the tree.' I love sharing these energies with others,
bringing them more deeply in touch with their own soul
connection creativity and power."

About the Teachings: The Sacred Geometry of Light.
It began as a powerful journey into sacred sites in the
deserts of the Southwest. Drawn by an irrepressible inner
calling, I followed the inner voice as it led me through an
amazing adventure. The experiences of that journey
shattered my preconceptions of the nature of the world.
Little did I know that the real journey had just begun.

When I returned home I began a series of paintings of
these mysterious places. The images came through with
great power and urgency and contained overlays of
universal symbols and geometric forms of light whose
message lay deep within my awakening consciousness. As
I completed the series of paintings, I was in meditation
asking for titles for an upcoming exhibition. Rather than
receiving titles, I entered into a powerful visionary experience that lasted many hours. As I encountered each
geometric lightform, I received information for its uses —
deep inner processes, complete with breath practices and
Egyptian mantras and an understanding of their meanings.
Later research into Egyptian symbolism confirmed the
accuracy of these meanings. Over the next year the trans-
missions broadened and deepened, becoming a system of
healing and spiritual growth. I knew deeply that this work
was a gift of Spirit and through years of practice and
teaching of these methods, I have come to honor the sharing
of these gifts. I am often deeply moved by the power and
beauty of lightforms and how they can help others break
through personal barriers.

The meditations are taught in three levels and cover a wide range of spiritual development: expanding inner vision, manifesting from your highest intentions, alignment with soul purpose and healing practices for yourself and others. Beginning with personal healing, the work expands out into a planetary context for healing in the universal grid. With use these powerful processes become a part of your internal "tool kit," expanding your consciousness and bringing peace and harmony into your world. A practical workbook of the meditations helps you to continue the process on your own.

Benefits:
- Development of sensory perception, psychic awareness, healing, manifesting, past-life and inter-dimensional understanding and a deepening awareness of universal power.
- Discovery of how sacred geometry affects our daily life.
- Hands-on tools for clearing, inner healing and expanding personal awareness.

Reiki Training and Mastership: Reiki means "intelligent universal life force" and is an ancient healing art practiced thousands of years ago in many parts of Asia. Reiki is experienced as a gentle flow of energy passing through the hands of the practitioner, balancing the mind, energy field and physical body, bringing deep peace and relaxation. Reiki is not a religion. There is no dogma or ideology and it is not tied to any spiritual belief system.

As a certified Usui Reiki Master, I teach traditional Reiki levels I and II, and work with individuals interested in training for Reiki Mastership. My lineage is derived through three original masters taught by Mrs. Takata and fees vary according to individual needs. Reiki is a wonderful place to begin your spiritual journey in the world of energy awareness and healing. For those already developed in your healing work, this will deepen and expand your existing practice.

Benefits:
- Deep relaxation, energy alignment and alleviation or lessening of physical pain.
- Attunement to the Reiki energy.
- Ability to help heal self and others, distance healing.
- New ways of bringing positive energy to difficult situations.

Shiva Shakti Yoga: The Teachings of Swami Kaleswar. A system of spiritual growth and healing given by direct transmission from the Indian yogic master Swami Kaleswar in Penukonda, A. P. India.

This powerful work is directly translated from ancient Sanskrit texts. These rare palm leaf books are many hundreds of years old, passed on from saint to saint for generations. They contain secret techniques and mantras for healing, supernatural and siddhic powers and the realization of God. Swami Kaleswar has given these teachings to a circle of students to teach these powerful mantras in the West. I am deeply honored to be able to bring these teachings to the Portland area. It includes:

- The Five Elements Course
- Brahma Kundalini
- The Sri Chakra

Recommended for the serious spiritual seeker who is drawn to the Eastern path and is willing to devote a daily period of time to meditation and mantra practice.

Benefits:
- Inner peace and bliss.
- Clearing and cleansing of blocks to spiritual development.
- Powerful healing abilities for yourself and others.
- Increased abilities to connect with higher powers.

(*) Frost, Kathy
(503) 492-9421
(888) 861-2626
Gresham, Oregon
crystalclarity@webtv.net

Psychic • Teacher

I became aware of my skills at an early age when I was able to see angels, spirits, guides and fairy lights. It was only through the guidance of my maternal grandmother that I became aware that not everyone saw or wanted to see angels, guides and other spirits. As I advanced in age, I learned when and where to share with a person their own information, from their guidance on a personal basis. After studying with a group in Southern California, I became a professional reader in 1992. My intention is to assist others in their own lives and healing those issues that need their personal attention.

I work in the clear light of Spirit. Integrity and accurate information is always my full intent for all readings.

My main focus is to connect people to their own infor- mation, via their guidance, personal Spirit and angelic host, which accompanies all of us in our travels through this life.

Any and all information, if it is appropriate at the time, will given regarding anything from health, prosperity, relationships, property, past life influences and choices available to each person at that time.

Whatever is primary for each person at the time of the reading is what he or she will receive. I am the reader and mouthpiece for their guidance and Spirit. I will be given visions, issues, revealed past life influences and connections to your higher information.

I also offer classes in metaphysics for the beginner and directions for the more advanced to assist you in your personal spiritual growth.

Each session is audio taped and lasts from 45 minutes to an hour and a half.

Crystal reading and toning by voice or toning bowls are also available.

Gardner, Judy
Waldport, Oregon
(541) 563-3359

Palmistry • Teacher • Mandalas

Palmistry. Judy is a very well-known and respected palmist and palm teacher who has read hands for many years in the United States and Egypt. Her training was at the International Institute of Hand Analysis in California, where she underwent two years of intensive training and received her certification as a palmist. She continued her studies by doing research with HIV-positive recovering addicts and studying all books on palmistry that have been available. Judy also loves sharing information with her peers. Most of her training is based on medical research of the hands.

Judy believes that palmistry is both scientific and spiritual because lines in the hands are a result of brain-directed activity. Our thoughts — which are a result of our desires, hopes, and attitudes — are transmitted through these lines. Also a careful study of hand shapes, skin texture, fingers and fingerprints gives us even more information. In fact, our hands reveal who we are and how we function and relate in the world through our emotions, thoughts and actions. Our gifts, talents, challenges, and our life purpose is clearly recorded in our hand. The hand is a road map to our life's journey.

Judy's love for people and her ability to use palmistry as a spiritual tool for guidance and healing is why Judy continues to be devoted to the science of palmistry.

Palmistry can change your life in many wonderful ways.

Judy offers readings for individuals, couples, businesses, groups and parties, and she is available to teach in your area. Judy has an office in Portland and is a regular reader at New Renaissance Bookstore one weekend per month. Another Portland location for Judy is the Lifeways Psychic Expo held in New Montgomery Park in the fall and spring of each year. Other locations include Crystal Wizard in Lincoln City, Mystic Mountain Bookstore in Corvallis (also one weekend per month), By the Sea Books in Yachats and her home in Waldport, Oregon. For appointments and schedules, call her at the above number.

Mandalas. Judy invites you to transform your life through her classes, "Mandala Magic." Discover the artist within.

Mandalas are circular paintings or drawings that have appeared on ancient cave walls and rocks in Africa, America and Europe. They have also been used through the world in sacred and inspired art and literature for centuries. They have been used in all cultures. Mandalas have long been seen as images of vision and revelation. In contemporary times they are very often used as tools for growth, change, healing and insight. Carl Jung, the eminent psychologist, worked with mandalas both personally and with his patients. He equated this circular design with the center or self in its movement toward wholeness and individuation.

Judy has been painting and teaching mandala art for many years and through her experience has realized that this art form is one of the most powerful and transformational spiritual tools that we can use for ourselves.

Judy has worked with HIV-positive recovering addicts using mandala art therapy with wonderful results. She has also taught mandala art for Stebbins Institute and for school districts in California and has appeared on TV with her mandalas. Judy offers private lessons at her home on the Oregon Coast, and classes for groups in Oregon and California.

Chakra Studies. Judy also offers a chakra series for total transformation as the students work with one chakra per month. Chakras are spinning vortices of energy in our body and we have seven of them. To reach and maintain excellent health — mentally, physically, emotionally and spiritually — all chakras must be open, clear and have energy flowing through. The more energy we allow to flow, the healthier we are.

Questions we have about fears, limitations, and strengths will be answered for you as you take this exciting and pleasurable journey into self-discovery. From this stronger connection to your core of being you will be able to stay centered in your power, bringing about more joy and fulfillment in your life.

No art experience necessary. For more information, call the telephone number above.

Gardner, Ralph
Portland, Oregon
273-6362 (voice mail)
222-4868 (office)

Clairvoyant • Reiki • Past-Life Regressionist • Channel

My world opened up on December 20, 1968, when the car I was driving spun on ice at 60 mph and rolled over several times, flipping once in the air. In those moments, I experienced myself being detached from the accident, almost separate from what was happening. During the spin, I felt a vague sense of movement, though my body was perfectly still with my hands gently gripping the steering wheel. I couldn't move my body and immediately realized I wasn't affected by centrifugal force when the car was spinning. At the same time I was able to see the inside of the car clearly but looking outside through the windshield; I could only see pure white. It was after 7 p.m. and all the outside was coated with snow.

The next moment I realized the car was overturning, but only noticed a slight feeling of movement, kind of a gentle swaying. Again I tried to see through the window but only pure white was visible. Then in the next moment the car had stopped and was upright. I realized this as I was

still attempting to see through the white light. In what
seemed like several seconds, what could only be described
as a veil began to lift, and I saw the car as it really was:
wrecked. All the glass had popped out and I was able to get
out through the driver's side door. I brushed myself off as if
I had just gotten up from sitting on the ground, and realized
that I had no injuries or shock. The area around me was
bright because of the snow, and visibility was perfect,
which led me to wondering about what I was experiencing
around my car during the accident.

Traffic had come to a dead stop to witness what was
happening and the couple who drove me into the small town
of Mojave were astounded that I was able to walk away. It
was these people who described to me how the car had spun
around several times, rolled and flipped over. This
confirmed what I had felt, and the state policeman said that
no one ever survives this type of impact collision. It was
becoming clear to me then, and more so over the years, the
true nature of the Light and how it had surrounded me that
day.

Some people who come away with experiences of
seeing the Light, (such as a moving through a tunnel of light
and communicating with transcended beings) return with a
heightened sense of awareness and gifts of psychic ability. I
thought I had received none of these. Well, as I have
realized over the years, especially recently, that was not
exactly true.

After several years of involvement in a relatively
unknown fraternal order known as the Order of the Rose
Cross (Rosicrucian), I began a personal process of healing
in mid-1989. Over the next few years, I went through two
clairvoyant training programs, a healing class, and received
my Reiki Master degree. The last two years have been the

most profound regarding the expression and development of my healing gifts. In May, 1996, I began to channel in higher vibrational light energies that were finer in nature than Reiki. I spent time working with different people to discern the nature of what these "new" energies were about. In combination with some regression techniques and NLP (neuro-linguistic programming), I began to integrate all the various tools into a more specific process. Included in that is a process I call — and termed by others — shamanic breathwork, which injects light energy very rapidly into the body and moves out "dark" energy (congestion of various energies and emotional blockages) very quickly.

A typical session with me involves what I simply call past-live regression healing. It begins with an alignment process that involves bringing in light energy through the body and the chakras. This allows an energetic bonding and helps the person receiving the to be able to begin relaxing deeply and enter into a light state of meditation (light trance). This can also be understood as a centering process that builds rapport and trust. It is during this phase that I can address any physical concerns that are ongoing and then begin to discuss the emotional and feeling aspects of current issues. At this point, I look at the "story" that is being described and guide the client gently into their feelings. By using a guided visual process, we are able to safely and easily go back in time, be it this life or past life, to the time and moment when the pattern/belief system was created. It is important to note that we are multi-dimensional beings and that I refer to all parts, be it childhood or some point in past lives, as "aspects." We are a composite of thousands of aspects, not only all the lives we have ever lived, but also the many we are living in this alone, be it child, adolescent, or adult.

As we begin to have a visual of a scene, we identify the connection, and if the experience is a traumatic one — as they often are — we immediately bring the aspect of that life into a safe, separate space. This immediately disconnects the emotional charge of that moment and, in turn, allows us to bring calm and comfort, as well as understanding and joy to the aspect. What follows is the continuation of my channeling in different levels of Light energy that allows the aspect and the client to become part of a larger healing process that affects all past generations and with any Soul with whom they have created karma. This group healing is highly instrumental to the client's being free from old pattern/belief systems. Already the client will have been experiencing powerful heart openings that bring in continuous waves of peace, joy, and a deep sense of connection with their own spirit and Higher Self. The latter part of the session involves the use of some NLP techniques that allow an integration of the current "self" with all the past "aspects" of the whole self.

What is key for all of us is to understand is the what and why of healing. Becoming whole is what healing is attempting to do. The why of healing is to facilitate our pathway on the journey to enlightenment or unity consciousness. To accomplish this is the act of embracing the shadow side of our personal self. This can be a daunting task and the resistance to feeling this level of pain is high for anyone, yet this path is the "shortcut" to freedom of the soul, free from the bonds of ego patterns and suffering.

This process I have developed is a powerfully gentle one that brings rapid personal growth and some immediate relief for both physical and emotional issues. Other expected results this experience will bring to you are the following:

- release of emotional blocks and negative belief systems
- relief of physical and emotional pain, stress and tension
- improved clarity and focus, and a sense of purpose
- heightened self-awareness and lightness of being
- chakra alignment and clearing.

Shedding the past, the act of letting go of attachments to beliefs and perceptions, is what will bring fulfillment to our lives. It is the act of living in the present moment. This brings in light: peace, love and lots of joy.

Garvey, Mary, LMT
A Sanctuary for Healing and
Present Moment Seminars
Portland, Oregon
(503) 288-4502

Healer • Teacher

I have been practicing massage and healing work for the past nine years. I was first drawn to this work from the perspective of a dancer. I had studied various forms of dance, yoga, and meditation when I began my massage practice. As a dancer I have a respect for the body and movement that has always been an integral part of my life. Dance, for me, has become a metaphor for magic and communing with the divine. I experience healing work in much the same way. The body's own natural intelligence speaks to us about what it needs, if only we will listen. It is always so incredible to be able to assist people in the process of letting go and discovering whatever needs to be revealed.

Within a year of practicing massage I began to receive strong currents of energy that have always felt like the Holy Mother Mary. This was at first quite a strange experience given that I was never particularly religious and was not raised with much knowledge of her. As my work evolved I would receive images and colors that I would use as I massaged my clients, and as I've become more confidant and trusting I've been able to share these impressions with people more openly.

Three years ago I introduced Craniosacral therapy to my work which has added a dimension of depth and relaxation that has truly been profound. Using sound, visualization, chakra clearing and energy balancing in addition to various forms of massage (Swedish, deep tissue, acupressure, and trigger point therapy) I also work with stones, crystals and vibrational healing such as flower essences and aromatherapy.

In a typical session I incorporate protection, release, clearing and guidance through intuition and connection with the Masters, angels and beings of Light that are constantly present as our true nature is. My intention is to use the gifts I have been given to help people feel more at peace, clear and in touch with their spirit. My intuition is experienced through empathy as it is quite natural for me to feel people's feelings, both physically and emotionally, and to facilitate healing from this perspective.

In addition to one-on-one healing I am currently teaching stress reduction workshops in business as well as yoga, meditation and relaxation.

(*) Geldon, Dianne
Beaverton, Oregon
(503) 646-2212

Medical Intuitive • Healer

Diane is a gifted medical intuitive. By examining your spiritual body, she diagnoses ailments — physical, mental, spiritual — and recommends herbal or nutritional treatments. She sees the emotional causes (either from past lives or earlier in this life) of many chronic illnesses.

Diana also does energy work in response to what she sees in your health analysis. She is able to clear out energy blockages from the afflicted area, which speeds up the healing process, and is particularly effective with ailments which have arisen out of emotional trauma.

Getten, Mary
Friday Harbor, Washington
(360) 378-4625

Telepathic Animal Communicator • Consultant

Mary J. Getten is a Telepathic Animal Communicator and Consultant. Telepathic communication can help you understand your animals better, resolve behavior problems and address important issues such as:

- Why doesn't my cat use the litter box?
- My elderly dog is ill. Is she ready to leave the world?
- How can our relationship be harmonious?
- What do my pets want or need?

Mary will converse with your pets so that you can understand each other's points of view. Problem behavior is usually a cry for help and speaking to your pet through this experienced, compassionate communicator can help you understand and often solve the problem. She may also suggest flower essences, dietary changes, energy work, body massage or other healing techniques to help your pet.

Ms. Getten began studying telepathic communication in 1988 and opened her consulting practice in 1996. She does consultations on the phone. When making an appointment, Mary will discuss the problem or issue with you and ask that you make a list of questions. During the consultation, you will ask Mary a question, she will then speak with the animal telepathically and relay the answer to you. This gives you the opportunity to speak to the animal through her and follow up with additional questions or clarification. Half-hour consultations are reasonably priced and most issues can be dealt with in that amount of time.

In addition to her animal consulting, Mary works extensively with marine mammals and other wildlife. She is a coordinator of the San Juan County Marine Mammal Stranding Network, a designated coordinator of wildlife rescue for Islands Oil Spill Association and a staff member at Wolf Hollow Wildlife Rehabilitation Center, all on San Juan Island in Washington State. Since 1991, she has been a naturalist on whale watch cruises that specialize in orcas.

Mary is the author of *The Orca Pocket Guide* published by EZ Nature Books in 1996. She is currently writing a book with fellow communicator Raphaela Pope about orcas from their perspective by interviewing wild and captive whales. This book, titled *Voice of the Whales: Conversations with an Orca Elder,* should be available in bookstores in 1999.

Mary has solved problems for clients throughout the United States and Canada. She has consulted with everything from slugs to whales. Hear what your animal friend has been trying to tell you for years.

Karen Hamel-Noble
Stillwater, Oklahoma
(405) 377-2668
http://www.cyberhorse.com/Noble.

Equine Parapsychologist

Karen Hamel-Noble, an Equine Parapsychologist with a gift of healing, has been working with horses and other animals for 16 years. The purpose and goal of her gift is to bring balance back to body, mind, and soul. The main part of her work is metaphysically done; or, in other terms, absent healing. She has clients all over the U. S. and Canada, as well as Argentina and Ireland.

The information required for a reading for a horse, for example, is: registration number, birthday, sex, color, and registration. If that information is not available, she will need a picture and a complete description.

Karen has had the honor of being in the book *The Top 100 Psychics of America*. She is the author of Through These Your Hands With Mind. She has been on radio and TV interviews and the subject of numerous magazine and newspaper articles. Karen lectures and puts on clinics with her husband Less, who raises and trains registered quarter-horses.

Having a reading done for your pet helps you have an understanding of what they need as an individual to keep

them in balance — body, mind and soul — in a natural and
healthy way.

   If you feel the need to have a reading done for your
pet or horse, you may contact Karen through the phone
number or website listed above. If you are interested in her
book, you may contact her at this address: Route 6 Box 210,
Stillwater, OK 74074.

Hammond-Newman, Mary
M.A.
The Heart Center
Salem, Or.
503-585-8992

Past Life Therapist • Intuitive • Healer • Spiritual Counselor • Teacher • Consultant

The Journey

I can trace my journey to my current practice of past life therapy and soul work with people back 37 life times ago where I have discovered a life when I taught healing arts to others, and also to this life's loving mother and grandmother who bountifully fed my quest for creativity, imagining, and spirituality. My spiritual quest has been closely linked with my professional calling. For three decades I have supported others in their seeking as a teacher, counselor, and healer. Visions, voices and knowings began many decades before I knew what to do with them. In the last decade I have learned simply to share them with the understanding that the intuitive world is fluid. Psychic information should not replace Spirit's guidance, and should be coupled with other levels of decision making (i.e., the physical, mental, practical, and financial). As the vibrations of the planet support many in their evolution into the new millennium, I am also supported to know and to

seek at levels I had not imagined. I invite you to join me in
this realm.

The Work

You can come to me to curiously or seriously explore
past lives. People do past life work to find out more about
certain aspects of themselves, to discover and retrieve gifts
previously held, or because they have past life memories or
fragments of memories (although this is not true for the
majority of my clients). People also do past life work to
heal relationships, depression, abuse, anxiety, trauma, or
chronic physical illness. This can take one session or ten-
plus sessions depending on the complexity of the issues.
You can expect to co-create with me your healing journey
using past life regression and Healing from the Body Level
Up for more complex issues. Experiencing a past life is
much like revisiting a dream. While there I will guide you
with specific techniques for healing, or retrieving information or gifts. I will also share intuitive awarenesses as they
come to me, or you can ask questions of me to ask for
guidance for you. Your journey might also include self-
administered acupressure, kinesiology (muscle testing),
dream work, sand tray therapy, imagery, breathwork, journaling, creative expression, rituals, or ceremony. You will
discover more of the best of you and finally heal illness or
troublesome areas of your life.

Women of Power

Over a period of several hundred years potentially
millions of powerful women were labeled witches and
killed for their gifts. There are also countless other lives
and times when women have given up their power or had it
stripped from them. It is deeply moving for women to

return to these lives that long to be healed and retrieve personal and community power as well as the gifts of intuitive/psychic knowing, teaching, energy work, hands on healing, nursing, midwifery, channeling, writing etc. This work contributes to creating the feminine spiritual energy needed for healing in the new millennium. This work can also be done in groups of women.

Children's Past Lives

Children between the ages of two and five may spontaneously have past life memories (Bowman, '97). I am available to the families of these children to teach them how to reduce the trauma of these memories as well as to help parents make sense of these stories. Older children can easily participate in past life regression for the same benefits that adults achieve. Families can revisit a past life together to better clarify their purpose for coming together again and bring healing to their present life together.

Soul's Purpose

Individually or in my Soul's Purpose class you can explore the reasons for your soul's existence. Together we use imagery, NLP timeline, journaling and sharing to heal the blocks to our soul achieving it's purpose. You then will get support for developing a plan to get your life on track so that you can live the life that Spirit intends for you.

Hatfield, Mary, M.A.
Licensed Professional Counselor
Portland, Oregon
242-0602 office

Healer • Counselor

The Hawaiian Healing Circle: I lived in Hawaii for five years, from 1983 to 1988, and had the opportunity to study Hawaiian Healing and Spirituality with Kahiliopua. Kahiliopua was the student of Auntie Emma de Fries, and also her hanai (adopted) daughter. Auntie Emma was highly respected among Hawaiians as a spiritual leader in tune with nature. She was honored as a "Living Treasure of Hawaii" in 1979 for her teaching of ancient Hawaiian culture. She died in 1980.

The form of healing taught to me is meditative in nature, and is done in a group. While meditating, we use the energies of natural elements (sunshine, wind, rain water, sea water and earth) for healing.

Kahiliopua has given me permission to teach what I have learned. I am offering both a workshop (3 hours) and an ongoing group for those who want to continue to practice and deepen their understanding.

Dreamwork - Consultation and Classes: I offer private dreamwork sessions, and also an eight-session class in dreamwork. Curriculum materials have been developed from the work of C.G. Jung, Robert Moss, Strephon Kaplan-Williams and Gayle Delaney.

Dreamwork tools include association and amplification, Gestalt work, grounding of the dream imagery through artwork and action, and dream "re-entry" using light trance. Students become familiar with the symbolic language of their dreams, and learn to discover whether their dreams are trying to inform, heal, teach, or are moving them to change something in their lives.

For information, please call the number above.

Heinz, Rita, LCSW
Portland, Oregon
(503) 234-5583

Sensitive • Empath • Counselor

My intuitive abilities have developed gradually over the course of 25 years as a psychotherapist and a lifetime of Western and Eastern spiritual practice. I have done my own deep psychological healing work and have turned old wrenching pain into great blessings. I continue to learn to find the rich spiritual opportunities in all the facts of my life.

I welcome those who place spiritual growth as their primary goal in life. I work with people, usually over a period of several sessions, to release pain and limitations, expand into their greater capacity for peace and love, and magnetize to themselves their highest good. I might incorporate methods such as guided imagery, thought field therapy, and healing energy transmission. I begin and end the session with a prayer which honors each individual's spiritual path.

I am compassionate, not preachy; warm, easy to talk to. I can often put subconscious thoughts, beliefs and feelings into words so that one may choose what to do with them. I help to create stillness, so that each may access his/her own intuitive, divinely guided direction. I teach each individual how to continue this process.

Some other facets of my work include:

- An 8-week Forgiveness Group
- A 4-week Meditation Group.

Call for dates. If the client is experiencing financial limitation, fees may be adjusted. My location is easily accessible in the Portland area.

Hill, Judith
Portland, Oregon
(503) 234-6633 (Portland Office)
(503) 224-4929 (New Renaissance
Bookshop)

Vocational Astrologer

Biography: Judith A. Hill is a second-generation astrologer with 30 years of consulting experience. She has served as the Educational Director for the San Francisco NCGR and as a faculty member of the Institute for Stellar Influence Studies. She is author of *The Astrological Body Types: Face Form & Expression,* (Stellium Press, 1993); *Vocational Astrology,* (Borderland Sciences, 1998); and *The Part of Fortune in Astrology,* (Stellium Press, 1998). Her first book has achieved Russian and Lettish language publications.

Perhaps best known for her innovative work in astrological research, she has lectured at many conferences both inside and outside of the astrological community. Her international publications of scientific research: "The Mars-Redhead Link", with J. Thompson, and "The Regional Factor in Planetary - Seismic Correlation", with M. Polit, have been widely acclaimed as major breakthroughs in the field of astrological research. Her astrological research work was featured on the television show "Strange Universe."

Judith achieved 100 percent accuracy in the matching of five anonymous birth charts to biographies in a 1986 skeptic-designed NCGR-sponsored contest. For many years she authored the innovative series "Astrology, Philosophy of Time and Space" for Sufism magazine. Judith runs a full-time consulting practice in Portland, Oregon, and specializes in Vocational Astrology.

Background: Judith began her astrological studies at the age of 10. As a lifetime astrologer, she has worked with a variety of astrological genres including ancient Greek, Vedic and Elizabethan. She has extensive consulting and teaching experience in several astrological specialty branches including: Horary (questions), Electional (timing selections), Medical, Transit, Mundane (world), Natal, Relationship, Locality and Vocational. Augmenting studies include: physiognomy, palmistry, comparative religion and spirituality, anthropology, numerology, feng shui, music, psychology, herbology, upaye (Vedic art of astrological gem prescription), world history, astrological history, biography, science writing, research methodology, and illustration.

The reading: Your 90-minute, taped, vocational reading opens with the presentation of a beautiful hand-drawn copy of your planetary birth chart. In the first half-hour, Judith will describe your abilities and suggest specific careers. Vocational difficulties will also be discussed. There is nothing vague about the reading — Judith is known for her precision and specificity. Her language is down to earth and practical. Judith prepares herself with a two-hour detailed noted study of your chart prior to your actual reading.

The second half-hour is time for your input. Judith compares suggested careers for three factors: talent, happiness, and profitability. Typical vocational questions can be addressed such as: "What branch of medicine should I go into?"; "Should I take a business partner or work solo?"; "What products would be the most lucrative for me?"; "When should I open the new business?" If you are already in a satisfying career, you may still benefit from the vocational and business tips available in your natal, progressed and transit charts. Judith has also worked with employers in the selection of employees.

Career timing and cycles are reviewed in the final half-hour of the reading. In sum, you can expect to receive a thorough outline of your talents, compatible careers and vocational timing. Problems are addressed and "antidotes" suggested. Additional questions you may have regarding any career-related topic can be addressed within the session.

Appointments. Taped in-person sessions, taped phone sessions, and taped readings are all available. Because of the careful preparation required for each reading, combined with Judith's popularity, spaces are limited. Be sure to call three to four months in advance of when you wish to arrange your appointment.

James, Marc
Gresham, Oregon
(503) 663-1188
marcjames@juno.com

Astrology • Numerology • Reiki • Tarot

I was introduced to astrology, numerology and Tarot at age 9. In 1987 I began a four-year sabbatical to study metaphysics. In that time I researched 400 volumes of astrology. In 1991 I became the In-House Astrologer for Aurora Books in Portland and The Crystal Wizard in Seattle. (I strongly advised both to incorporate their businesses to give them new birth times and dates. They didn't. They're both closed today.)

I have been through the Silva Mind Control class and the Monroe Institute's Human Plus training. I am a Reiki Master and a certified hypnotherapist.

While it is difficult to describe what a "typical" session might be like, I can say that I spend two to three hours setting up several charts (natal, secondary progressed, solar arc directions, solar return, relocation if required, and Vedic) preparing for our counseling session.

As a result of our session, you will understand your "contract with God;" that is, what you agreed to be and do. The type of relationships you attract, the career you are best

suited for and when you can expect and plan for your
success. Then from your Vedic chart I will show you your
specific remedial techniques that will improve your circumstances.

If you are indigent, there is no charge.

There are two general remedial techniques that you
can put to use right away to remove negative karma and
improve your circumstances:

1. Every morning, after bath, shower or at least
   washing hands and face, and before you eat or drink,
   put out a fresh bowl of water for the birds. You may
   also give birdseed.
2. Help/be of service to old, aged and needy people
   and parents and/or parents-in-law.

Jurdan, Morgan
Amboy, Washington
(360) 247-5310
morgine@hotmail.com

Telepathic Animal Communications

My name is Morgine. I am a Telepathic Animal Communicator. Simply put, I carry on a two-way conversation with animals. This is not a special psychic gift; it is something anyone with the desire can learn to do. Do you love animals and desire to share your own feelings and concerns with them? Would you like to hear about their own personal viewpoints and learn how to understand them better, help with illnesses, behavior problems, moving, dying and more? Telepathy is something that occurs naturally, and when you can be present, open, and free from judgments and assumptions, you can use it consciously and easily. You can open new doorways in your life and expand your awareness. I offer phone consultations, presentations, lectures, and workshops. Please feel free to call me with your questions regarding any of these.

I have been working in the field of communication for many years. I have trained with Penelope Smith, Samantha Khury, Dorothy Maclean, Ken Page, Danaan Parry and others. I am featured in a book called *Communicating With*

Animals by Arthur Myers. I incorporate a variety of healing
techniques into what I do, including energy work, flower
essences, nature conings, and more. I love what I do and do
it with love, for we are all One, and I believe wisdom often
lies where we least expect it. Discover something new
today.

Kidd, MaryJean, M.S.
Portland, Oregon
(503) 288-7633
MKIDD4728@aol.com

Astrology.

Using her background in psychology, education, alternative healing and astrology, MaryJean helps clients understand their own life patterns and spiritual paths. She also offers tools to aid in the clearing of these patterns so that clients are better able to follow their paths. Perceptive, supportive, and compassionate guidance are provided to each client as MaryJean works with them to achieve their goals.

Astrology: A typical astrological session will focus on potentials and challenges found in the birth chart which may be activated during the current times. A review of the upcoming year is given, along with insight into the psycho-spiritual process of the year. MaryJean provides validation, perspective, and direction. Specific questions from the client are answered. Some clients choose to have a session focus on an area of life such as career, relationship, business ventures, locality, soul lessons, karmic issues, etc. Clients leave with a strong sense of direction and a feeling of re-connection with their path.

Counseling: Counseling sessions often involve the use of contemporary healing techniques such as Healing from the Body Level Up™, Thought Field Therapy ™, and Reiki. MaryJean's approach to working with clients is aimed at empowering clients and providing the most efficient and effective ways of releasing and resolving emotional and spiritual issues. Goals are identified and then blocks to achieving these goals are removed. Clients are then able to successfully work toward creating a life that is more satisfying.

A full-time professional astrologer, counselor and Reiki Master with over 15 years of experience, MaryJean offers consultations as well as ongoing counseling to individuals, couples, families and businesses. Sessions are either in-person or over the phone. She teaches workshops and classes on astrology, both for the general public and students of astrology. Chart rectification (for those with no accurate birth time) is offered. Chart services, astrology reports and software are also available.

Koch, Robert A
760 N.W. Broken Arrow Road
Bend, Oregon 97701-9037
Phone: 541-318-0248
Web site:
http://www.robertkoch.com
E-mail: rk@robertkoch.com

Vedic Astrology

Robert A Koch has been a practitioner of the predictive art of Vedic astrology for more than fifteen years. In his work, he draws upon experience gained from his twenty years as a Vedic monk. His teacher, sri Sriman A. C. Bhaktivedanta swami, is revered as one of the most prolific teachers of Vedic thought in the modern age.

Vedic astrology (called *Jyotish,* or the science of light) comes to us from India since times pre-dating the Christian era. Vedic astrology assumes the law of karma, which states that a human being lives and works within certain parameters created by actions performed in prior lifetimes. Thus it is generally regarded as predictive in nature, as it can show when the results of such prior actions will come to fruition in the present life.

Robert traveled to India six times in the late 1970s, where he learned both Vedic scriptures and Sanskrit, and had first-hand experience of the culture founded upon its principles. In 1987, he left the monastic life, returned to America, and began his full-time professional practice of

Vedic astrology. His goal was to bring the Vedic teachings, particularly the practical readings of destiny through astrology, to people at a more personal level.

At present, Robert is doing full-time Vedic astrological consultations and teaching in Bend, Oregon. He is also currently working on a book entitled *Life and Longevity, As Seen Through the Vedic Horoscope,* which contains comprehensive research about determining life span through Vedic Astrology. He is also a regular contributing author to the prestigious *ACVA Journal* (American Council of Vedic Astrology). He is a founding as well as faculty member of the ACVA, and lectures regularly at its annual world symposiums on Vedic astrology.

Robert is a contributing author to an anthology on Vedic astrology entitled *Hindu Astrology Lessons,* edited by Richard Houck. Groundswell Press published the anthology in May 1997. This book is a compilation of articles written by the country's most prominent Vedic astrologers. Robert's inclusion in this collection is testimony to his reputation.

Labay, Mary Lee
Bellevue/Seattle
(425) 455-1910 (phone and fax)
e-mail: marylee@w-link.net

Psychic • Counselor • Hypnotherapist • Past Life Regressionist

Mary Lee is a Certified Clinical Hypnotherapist and Registered Counselor. Specializing in past life regressions, a person can not only discover who they were in a previous lifetime, but also their purpose in life, spiritual lessons, communicate with their spirit guides, open their psychic abilities, and gain a deeper understanding of their relationships. These techniques are equally effective in facilitating the healing of chronic pain, addictions, disease, blocks, and other impediments to complete, positive life progress.

The techniques that Mary Lee uses are gentle and relaxing, leaving the client in complete control of the session. Expect to gain deep and intriguing insights into your own subconscious. Be prepared to empower yourself! It oftentimes only takes one session to initiate any desired behavioral changes.

Mary Lee has been facilitating regressions for over a decade and presently teaches the techniques to graduating hypnosis students at two separate schools in the Northwest. She also conducts two-day intensives for professional hypnotherapists desiring to improve their regression skills.

Mary Lee began studying astrology and Tarot in 1967 and became a professional reader in the mid-80's. Using Tarot, astrology, pendulum and clairvoyance, she is able to assist you in gaining full and accurate information concerning all areas of your life. Learn about the conditions and future of relationships, career, health, travel and more , and what you can do to improve these areas of your life.

After years of studying under a private spiritual teacher, Mary Lee now teaches metaphysical topics, both privately and in classes, and is a popular guest speaker. She is also a continuing education instructor at Bellevue Community College, near Seattle, giving workshops on Tarot, astrology and past life regressions. Mary Lee has been a longtime contributing author for New Times (Seattle) and Enlightenments (Ohio) and has a singles advice column in the Active Singles Life magazine available around the great Northwest.

Please contact her by phone or e-mail to set up your private, personal, confidential reading or hypnosis session. Empower yourself and take control of your future.

Lail, Esther
Boulder, Colorado
(303) 402-1905

Clairvoyant

What is clairvoyance? Clairvoyance literally means the ability to see clearly. It is a gift we all have and it can be developed just like exercising a muscle. Esther has a unique ability to see the aura or energy field around people. Clairvoyant reading is a visual method accessed while in a light trance. If there is a trick to being psychic, it is the ability to be neutral in relation to any belief. There are a variety of non-invasive psychic tools used to retrieve helpful information.

What are the benefits of getting a psychic reading? Being seen for who you are as spirit can be very healing. You can find out about your particular gifts and core challenges. Being validated for what you already know about yourself or a relationship can dispel self-doubt, confusion, and despair. Hearing about the subconscious beliefs involved can often produce a desirable shift. The way in which you hold on to the past can also change.

What is an aura healing? Aura healing is a non-intrusive way to remove foreign or unwanted energy such as discomfort or fatigue from the body. It can leave one feeling more present and alive.

In summary, the intent of this kind of psychic reading is to offer information while clearing the path for the client to find their own truth. This is an ethical, non-judgmental style of reading that allows the client the freedom to become more aware of his or her true self. Psychic reading and healing works well in person or on the telephone.

Esther also incorporates the use of Australian Bush Flower Essences in her practice. Flower essences are a powerful, safe form of vibrational healing. They are different from aromatherapy in that the essence of the flower is captured through a specific process which incorporates the vibrational power rather than the scent. These are a collection of 62 essences, made from wild flowers indigenous to Australia. They address a multitude of issues relating to modern-day life and are an effective form of natural healing.

Esther Lail has studied at the Marin Psychic Institute, San Raphael, California; is certified by the Earth School Institute, Portland, Oregon; and has 10 years of shaman training at Lynn Andrews' Joshua Tree Intensives, Joshua Tree, California. She has been doing readings for five years and also has a background in music.

Lambert Lewis
Gaston, Oregon
(503) 985-7268

Chocolate Cup Readings • Indian or Egyptian Tarot Card Readings • Therapeutic Touch.

Chocolate Cup Readings: Have a cup of chocolate with Lewis and when you are done, he will interpret the remaining chocolate pattern inside the cup. Information may include past, present and future indications.

Indian or Egyptian Tarot Card Readings: Your choice of two different decks, either Dakota-style Indian Tarot cards, or Ancient Egyptian Tarot cards, can guide you onto your spiritual path, and indicate the feelings around you. These readings give you a two- to three-month look into the future.

Therapeutic Touch: Therapeutic touch does not involve touch to the body, but through the aura or energy space around the body. Lewis will balance the chakras and smooth out any rough spots or problem areas in the aura. Afterwards you will feel relaxed and rebalanced.

Background: Lewis is a Native American whose lineage is from both the Makinaw and Willamette tribes. A recovered alcoholic for seven years now, Lewis has seen the light and is helping others on their spiritual path. He is in touch with his spiritual guides and may help you get in touch with yours also.

(*) Lee, Liza
Clackamas, Oregon
(503) 794-1277

Psychic • Past Life Regression • Hypnosis • Energy Balancing

I feel that everyone is born with intuition, but that during childhood many children or adolescents learn to block it, due to the influence of our parents, peers, or society. When I was a small child it was such a part of my "being" I believed that everyone experienced these "knowings" and abilities. As I grew older it did become necessary to learn how and when to block it to allow my concentration to develop in other areas. I was fortunate to have around me those who could help learn control and discernment and when to share with others what I "know." Along with this gift comes a sense of peace and a feeling of spiritual contentment and faith in knowing that I am never alone.

I was born in the Portland area and also spent several years in Washington before moving to Hawaii in the late 70's. While living in Hawaii, I participated in a number of psychic fairs. I also had the opportunity to create and appear with a colleague in a weekly live TV show on access cable called "Psychic Visions." It was truly amazing how many people we reached during that time. I've been back in the Portland area for two years now and occasionally appear on live radio programs doing readings and predictions.

I offer a few different services to my clients: psychic readings, hypnosis, past-life regression, and energy balancing. I can be reached at the above number and work from my office near Clackamas Town Center.

Psychic Reading. I like to do readings in person rather than on the phone, especially the first time with a client. I usually ask that you don't tell me anything about yourself beforehand because I would rather let my faith in the information coming through speak for itself. A normal reading (which I put on cassette tape) lasts half an hour and I'm able to give information about your relationships, friends and family, career and finances, and things to look forward to and possibly avoid during the next three months or so. I can also answer any specific questions that you may have. I feel that a psychic reading is fun and very informative, definitely a positive experience for my clients.

Hypnosis. I offer hypnosis as a tool for growth and positive change in the lives of my clients. A typical session lasts about an hour and is very relaxing. A cassette tape is made of the actual hypnosis part of the session and I urge my clients to take it home with them to reinforce the session in my office. Listening to the tape takes about 15-20 minutes, and five times a week is optimum for lasting change.

Past Life Regression. Past-life regression is a fascinating, workable tool to achieve emotional healing and is available for you to attain self mastery. It can assist in bringing you clarification and an understanding of your personal belief system and helps facilitate growth. You can learn to bring a sense of joy and happiness into your life. The session lasts 2-1/2 to 3 hours, and hypnosis is used to take you back to your own past.

Energy Balancing. Spiritual healing or energy balancing are offered to my clients as another tool for well-being. During this process the chakras are checked and repaired as necessary and the life energy restored to perfect balance. Spiritual energy and light is channeled during the session or sessions and sometimes crystals are used to facilitate healing. When completed, my clients feel a deep sense of well-being, peace, love and acceptance. Each session lasts about an hour.

Liu, Evelyn
Portland, Oregon
(503) 284-1108
e-mail: bretagne@earthlink.net

Healer • Reiki • Energy Worker

My path toward realizing my healing abilities began with a heart-wrenching divorce and a gigantic cosmic sledgehammer wake-up call. I went on a metaphysical journey and met a group of people who were developing their healing/psychic abilities. I was honored to be accepted into this group which provided a safe place to test/grow/explore my talent and skill. My greatest assistance came from a close friend who saw in me the power and potential and inspired me to accept my gift.

I act as a conduit for the life force energies. My method is a unique blend of Reiki and Therapeutic Touch. Working through my heart chakra, I enter an altered state and receive images and information regarding opportunities for growth.

People who have come to me and have found value in my work include those who seek respite from stress and anxiety; those who pursue a greater unity of spirit, mind and body, and those who desire transport to a place of calm and peace.

When you are drawn to my services, I establish the intent of wholeness and health for you within my heart and mind and allow the energy to flow through me to you. You, in turn, have great wisdom to accept and use what you need for your own healing physically, emotionally or spiritually.

The experiences and sensations you experience are highly personal and intimate. Some sense warmth, love and/or sweetness. Others sense energy surges. Significant images may appear. Some drop into a sleep, others go on a journey, but almost always, there is a feeling of calmness and having been in a deep state of relaxation at the end of the session.

In whatever way you experience my services, I trust that it will be what you need for your own growth and healing. Namaste.

Maaj
Starmuse
Chico, California
(530) 893-8825

*Astrology • Flower Diva • Nature's Kingdom
Practitioner • Certified Clairvoyant • Certified
Hypnotherapist • Psychic Healings • Aura Cleansings
• Universal Life Minister • Visionary Artist*

I began developing my psychic abilities as an infant,
from abuse. I found the fairie and flower diva kingdoms as
a very young child, as Nature was my true mother and
guide. I also learned to hear other frequencies with my inner
ear at this same time. I always say, first rose-petal mud-pies,
then flower essences and herbal tinctures into essential oils
and sound toning. All of which I use in my practice
regularly, except of course rose-petal mud-pies, which I use
for exceptional situations. I have made many flower
essences, and have a wonderful remedy for nerve-associ-
ated causes like herpes, all of which I mail order.

I found my way to astrology when I was reading
through the A's in the library. School was a safe place for
me to be when I was young — and old! In my practice I use
astrology like a golden or silver thread to ancient past and
distant future. Our astrological DNA is woven into patterns

on the eternal thread of time. That line holds our own unique story, our physical and spiritual life.

Over the years I have developed into a skilled interpreter, consultant, and weaver of these fine threads in time. Using astrology with my psychic and vibrational healing abilities, I am like a spiritual archeologist, dusting off the sands of time. I look into past, present, and future issues, exploring these individual tapestries of woven time. I watch for patterns that develop in collective and individual hopes, wishes, and dreams and help to weave them to their best advantage, strength and beauty in wholeness.

As a spiritual weaver, I check warp and woof. I begin shuttling on the loom of eternal time. Re-weaving worn threads of consciousness, slipped stitches of spiritual forgetfulness, and those k'nots' and w'holes' that keep us separate from our infinite unit.

My work as an astrologer, psychic and vibrational healer is a process consultation, using my skills, insights, and gifts to align the story that we as individuals weave into consciousness and create visually on the tapestry of our experience. Together we will weave each transit of experience as it connects to the next, adjusting the pattern and color of our beautiful expression into efficient function, durability, and joy-filled spiritual conscious awareness.

With light and love, may the winds of change be at your back and rainbows guide and light your journey into the future. Prosperity in all for all.

Macdonald, Liz
Angelwood
Seattle, Washington
(206) 729-2320
(800) 698-8985
www.angelwood.com
e-mail: love@angelwood.com

Channeled Angel Reading • Teacher

Liz has walked a spiritual path all her life. She has studied extensively with the Inner Peace Movement, and has been a member of the Edgar Cayce Foundation. In the spring of 1995 she began to automatically write. She found that literally one second it wasn't there and the next it was. Liz began sharing this gift at various psychic fairs, then in Northwest area bookstores by appointment. As word-of-mouth spread, she opened her own office and started the Angelwood Center with her business partner, Karen Cornell.

In a reading, Liz contacts your guardian angels through automatic writing. She encourages her clients to bring in written questions, and the range of information is unlimited: relationships, love, past lives, emotional healing, finances, career, health, sense of purpose — literally anything! Liz then reads aloud what is being written. She is what is called a clear channel and does not always know what the written information is talking about, as it does not come through her conscious knowledge. In addition, since she is separate, she may see, smell or hear things. The written information is then yours to keep to refer to when needed. If you have never had a reading of this type, you will find it very deep and constructive to your own personal growth.

Workshops: Using her hands-on method, Liz teaches workshops. "Tuning to Spiritual Guidance" teaches students to feel, touch and see energy. Participants also learn valuable techniques to connect with guidance. "Developing Psychic Abilities I" teaches various techniques on how to find your own unique ability. Each one of us has psychic abilities; just which ones? The student finds out in this class. "Developing Psychic Abilities II" goes more in-depth with your abilities and helps you discern how you get information and how you can improve upon it. Liz also teaches a class on automatic writing.

Parties: Having a party with a psychic is a lot of fun and sure to be a hit! Liz is available for parties, weddings or any special occasion.

She has been on radio stations "The Edge" and Hot 105.9 in Phoenix, and KKMO in Seattle, doing live on-air readings. Liz has been to Australia, New Zealand and Canada doing readings and teaching workshops and has a large clientele throughout the world.

Marcus, Deanna
The Self-Discovery Group
The Power of Clairvoyant Therapy
Portland, Oregon
(503) 236-5415
www.lifemotion.com
e-mail: deanna@lifemotion.com

Clairvoyant • Healer • Teacher

Clairvoyant Therapy is a powerful body of work. By unlocking and moving stagnant and blocked emotions, Clairvoyant Therapy is designed to build our energy systems, while closely examining our energy bodies and auras. Through this process we can change unhealthy subconscious patterns and behaviors.

Deanna has evolved a powerful and innovative body of work. Thousands have completed her courses in meditation, psychic healing and clairvoyance, and thousands more have experienced astounding transformations from their private sessions with her.

Certified in the teachings of the Washington Psychic Institute, and Berkeley Psychic Institute through the Church of Inner Light, Deanna has a deeply grounded understanding of metaphysical principles. This gives her the foundation to fully comprehend the human energy system — our vehicle for conscious creations.

Deanna's gift for earning our trust enables her to open the doors to our energy bodies to diagnose potentially debilitating issues and their sources with stunning accuracy. Her nurturing and compassionate style supports our individual process of healing and moves us beyond our most challenging issues. Deanna's passion and commitment to her work fuels her innovative, lighthearted and free-spirited approach.

Deanna will show you how to access pivotal events that have shaped your decision-making process. You will move beyond old limitations, gain clarity, and take positive steps to gain more of the life you want — spiritually, emotionally and physically.

For additional information on classes and workshops visit our Web site listed above.

Martin, Beverly
Light Dialogues
Hillsboro, Oregon
(503) 640-0753
e-mail: beverlynlp@aol.com

Healer • Channeler • Psychic

Originally from South Africa, Beverly has had 12 years of experience developing her clairvoyance and abilities as a medium.

Beverly has the ability to hear the voice of your Higher Self and the guidance which assists you to fulfill your life's purpose. The information that is given through her mediumship is loving and kind, refreshingly honest, deeply respectful of who you really are, as well as light-hearted and funny at times!

As a medium she is also able to make contact with loved ones who are in spirit. "This is a most rewarding part of my work. I have been privileged to facilitate communication between those who have passed over to the other side and their loved ones here. There have been tremendous healings as a result."

The readings will give perspective on past events which lead up to where you find yourself currently, a view on possible future outcomes and how you can adjust your course. Emphasis typically is on how you can fulfill your purpose and live the life you choose.

Though clients typically receive extremely helpful personal guidance, the readings are not "fortune telling." You will be given unique and helpful information in order to make the best choices, which are yours to make.

Those who are willing to be active participants in their lives unfolding, with curiosity and willingness to apply a spiritual perspective to everyday life, will find the readings a valuable source of guidance, encouragement and wisdom.

Classes: Beverly believes that all of us have the ability to hear the voice of our own hearts. In the "Light Dialogues" classes, she enjoys teaching you to access and trust your own intuition more fully.

NLP: Beverly is also a master practitioner of Neuro-Linguistic Programming and applies those skills assisting clients in the areas of health, well-being and personal effectiveness.

Masood, Marcia
West Linn, Oregon
(503) 657-9030

Healer

My gift in the intuitive arts is through healing. I think the word "healer" is a bit misleading, because I believe that ultimately we each heal ourselves, and that the healer acts to hold sacred space for the individual to take the journey to their innermost core. As a healer, I open myself to be a channel for my client's guides and my guides to do their work. People are drawn to me when they want to access their deeper truths, the essence of their consciousness, and to clear away the accumulated clutter.

As a client, you will want to wear comfortable, loose clothing for the session. You will remove your shoes and lie down on a massage table. If you choose, you may also sit up, or stand for the session. This work addresses all the levels of your field or aura, because your consciousness is reflected in your physical, emotional, mental and spiritual aspects of being. Wherever you have accumulated blocks or distortions in your understanding, there is a sense of dis-ease on one or more levels in the aura. My job is to assist in aligning all the levels of vibration to the note that is your soul. As you realign with your highest and deepest consciousness, you will experience healing.

My training has been in cranio-sacral therapy, polarity therapy, Reiki, and a four-year healing school. However, much of my understanding of healing has developed through remembering other lifetimes I have spent as a healer in various cultures using sound, color and vibration. Ultimately, I believe that love heals everything, and that we are all seeking to return to that state of being that is Love. The journey we take to get there is customized by each individual's consciousness, both light and shadow. And we always have choices.

Whatever your journey, I wish you blessings, and the courage to plumb the depths of your awareness to find your inner beauty and love.

McGinnis, Daniel
Blue Sky Healing Arts
Portland, OR 97218
(503) 248-1825
e-mail: bluskygy@concentric.net

Clairvoyant Counseling • Aura Readings • Energy Healing

Blue Sky Healing Arts is the name given to a dynamic counseling practice, offering aura readings, personal energy work, and classes in applied metaphysics, and meditation.

As a counselor, it is Daniel's intention to create an environment that supports the unfolding process of discovery. This means that there are no right or wrong answers — absolutes do not facilitate freedom. Daniel views his role as that of a guide, helping others to connect with their own resources in a way that makes sense to the individual. His skills and experience help the individual to better understand how and why perception and the freedom to choose became obscured.

The services offered in Daniel's practice do not usually include making predictions about the future. The future is a puzzle which we can only piece together by being in the moment. His work creates a new and powerful opportunity for his clients to be wholly and completely in the present, where the possibilities for the future can be seen and evaluated directly. For many of us, this is a transformational experience. Releasing ourselves from the burdens of the past brings new energy and clarity to the creative process; it is here that the future is constantly being born.

Compassionate and professional, Daniel helps people find answers they can use to create harmony and happiness in their career, relationships and personal development.

Blue Sky Healing Arts is located at 322 NW 5th Avenue, Suite #226, Portland, Oregon 97209. Daniel is available by phone and in person for individual sessions, classes and workshops.

(*) McQuary, Laurie
Management by Intuition
Lake Oswego, Oregon
(503) 636-1832

Psychic

Areas of expertise involve: Personal relationship issues, business clients, marketing ideas, comparison (psychically) to competition as well as employee/employer relationships.

Cases: missing persons, homicides are not charged for. Retainer fees are available for questions. International as well as national clients.

Laurie's style is direct, compassionate, but definitely to the point. No "method" of divination other than their name, birthdays are occasionally asked. Telephone sessions national as well as international, and all consultations are taped. Voted "Portland's Best" by the Willamette Week newspaper. No credit cards. Twenty-five years of established psychic work. Credibility statements are available on request.

Musgrave, Cassandra
Destination Light
Lake Oswego, Oregon
(503) 635-8898
e-mail:
destinationlight@worldnet.att.net

Clairvoyant • *Near-Death Experience Researcher*

Cassandra Musgrave is an expert intuitive, spiritual medium, animal psychic, healer, and near-death experience speaker who has been internationally active in metaphysics since her profound 1974 near-death experience. She has been featured in *Willamette Week's* "The Best of Portland 1998" and has been previously interviewed for Portland's "AM Northwest," "News Channel 8," and "Channel 12 News," as well as "Hard Copy," "Ancient Prophecies III" (NBC), and *Cosmopolitan* magazine. Her NDE research has been recently published in the *Journal of Near-Death Studies*.

Through her Portland, Oregon business, Destination Light, Cassandra teaches, lectures, and conducts hundreds of regressions and psychic readings (via phone or in person) in a climate of compassion and uncanny insight. "After my opening prayer and energetic clearing and balancing, before I take your questions, I relate what I see, sense, and feel about your personal, professional, and spiritual paths. I use clairvoyance, clairaudience, and skilled intuition to communicate with your High Self, angels, spirit guides, and loved ones unseen. I receive information in words, images, feelings, and through viewing photos. With gentle loving support, I assist in healing the past and creating clarity for your impending choices and decisions. With grounded practicality, I 'tune in' to your past lives and present and future trends for yourself/pets/loved ones. My intention is to activate and facilitate personal and planetary healing and transformation."

Orwen, Julia, M.A.
(360) 694-4550
Vancouver, WA

Telepathic Animal Counseling • *Aura Soma Color Consultations*

"The purpose of life is to live it, to taste experience to the utmost, to reach out eagerly and without fear for new and richer experience." — Eleanor Roosevelt

Julia Orwen, M.A., has practiced intuitive and healing arts for 16 years. She works with both people and animals, and provides a variety of services tailored to the needs of different types of clients. In her consultations, Julia draws from an eclectic background in mind-body counseling, hypnotherapy, shamanic practices, and vibrational healing techniques. Julia's compassion and intuitive gifts allow her to assist others with self-exploration and transformation in ways that encourage and honor individual processes of growth and development.

Individual or group sessions last approximately 1-1/2 hours, and consist of:

Telepathic Animal Counseling — Animals are here to teach us about unconditional love of ourselves, others and the planet. Julia uses telepathic communication to help people speak to their animal companions about issues of health, household relationships, behavior, mental and emotional states, and past history. Her intent is to provide individuals with supportive and practical guidance, and to help expand communication between people and their pets.

During a consultation Julia listens carefully to the problem situation outlined by clients and then tunes into the animal it get its point of view. Animals are usually delighted by the opportunity to express themselves, and solutions are arrived at quickly and easily through mutual love and understanding. In addition, Julia is able to assist the animal in releasing emotional blocks, disharmonies, and past traumas that are often the root cause of problems.

Aura Soma Color Consultations — Color is the key to understanding the soul at the deepest level. Julia uses Aura Soma, which is a unique form of color therapy combining the healing energies of color, plant extracts, and crystal essences. This system, consisting of an array of brilliantly colored oils in glass bottles, is based on the principle that you are the colors you choose. Aura Soma consultations are empowering and noninvasive. Clients intuitively select four colored bottles most relevant to them at the present time. This selection reflects their true aura, and all the beauty and potential that lies inside. Julia interprets the bottles to assist people in discovering their soul's purpose and goals, the challenges they face along their path, the gifts they possess, and future potentials and possibilities.

For additional information and fee schedules call the telephone number listed above.

O'Toole, Toni
Rock Creek, Oregon
(503) 645-3823

Intuitive • Clairvoyant • Clairaudient

I was raised with an openness to metaphysics and have always been most comfortable making choices based on my "gut feelings." Of course, we all do our best while living regular lives with all the challenges.

My awakening to the gifts of the spirits came in words and pictures and much joy. It is with joy and support that the spirits and your own Higher Self wish to communicate with you. I enjoy assisting in bringing forth the messages important to your own personal path. My readings involve clairvoyance, clairaudience and intuition to support you in understanding yourself. Phone readings may be arranged.

Palmer, Gina
Paws & Claws
Vista, California
(760) 630-0777

Background of Gift. Remembering my first experience with telepathic communication is one of my favorite
stories to share with students, and one of the most endearing
moments of my life.

I was studying in Yucatan, Mexico with Hunbatz Men,
Mayan Record Keeper and Elder. Five other students and
myself equaled seven, including Hunbatz. We had all been
traveling the sacred pyramids, learning about how to open
and work with their energy. Hunbatz introduced us to the
Mayan term "In Lak'ech." Roughly translated In Lak'ech
means, "I am another yourself." The basis of the term
includes everything and everyone as being equal to the
extent that no separation exists. In Lak'ech includes all
species, all forms of matter, stones, trees, etc.

After three days of working the energy within various
pyramids, Hunbatz prepared a special ceremony atop the
pyramid of Dzibilchaltun. He instructed us about the
aspects of a specific Mayan mantra, "Ol," and taught us
body position to hold while working this particular mudra.
The weather that day was balmy, and several cumulus
clouds hung lazily in the Yucatan sky, giving the impression

of gigantic cotton balls suspended inside of the tapestry of blue sky. Standing high upon the top of the pyramid allowed us to look out onto the vast lush greenscape which rolled out in every direction far below us, making the territory seem unending. Hunbatz asked us all to reach out and touch or make contact with one particular cloud. Pointing his index finger toward the sky, he instructed us to remain quiet and feel the cloud through a particular area of our body, located in between our breast bone, also known as our heart center. He asked us to feel the qualities of the cloud, the texture, color, size and direction in which it was located. We were then instructed to bring those qualities into ourselves through the area in between our eyebrows on our foreheads. He reminded us that the cloud too was In Lak'ech, and all manifestation is Spirit, or the Activity of God. Gunbatz told us that we were to ask the cloud to dissipate, for the purpose of verifying the loving connection we had all established with it. Imagine the body sensations one might have when a cloud literally disappears and vanishes right before your open eyes. That is precisely what happened in the location of the sky where the cloud had been only moments before.

Later, Hunbatz explained that the cloud had heard our intention and had simply agreed to participate with our request to dissipate. I could literally feel the communication inside of my body. I felt the connection the instant the cloud acknowledged our loving focus. Inside of my body, I felt the sensation of expansive presence similar to what one views while watching clouds gather energy in the sky as they increase and decrease in size. What most people have seen with their eyes, I felt inside of my body. Hunbatz explained that the principles he taught could be applied in communication with all of life, just as the teachings had been utilized in ancient times with his people, before telephones and technology had become the norm. He asked that we teach the rituals and use of telepathic communication to others upon our return home. Telepathic communication is everyone's birthright, and is only waiting to be reawakened, just as it had been with us that day.

What We Do Now. Working with the elements of Earth, Water, Air and our 13 animal companions (dove, quail, canine, feline, chicken, reptile and parakeet, who continue to be our teachers) while we work with students who come to the sanctuary to learn basic and advanced skills in animal communication. We offer group and private sessions, teaching on totem power animals and nature spirits. Private animal communication sessions are delivered by telephone to local and long distance clients, and can be tape recorded. We travel upon request delivering lectures, classes, public speaking and seminars. We keep in touch with students and clients through our quarterly newsletter, which we write and publish. The newsletter is available to anyone wishing to subscribe.

A consultation session realigns with the animal's viewpoint which in all cases will remain rooted in wholeness. The result of a thorough consultation session will be felt as a release and/or relief. At least that is what is often reported from clients/students. Our sessions and classes emphasize an expanded state of awareness, which frees the intellect/ego, and allows all concerned to take part in true knowingness, which can only be experienced from the heart. By allowing our consciousness to rest gently upon the consciousness of the beloved, be it animal, tree, or cloud, we find our true Self in the presence of the one on which our consciousness rests. When true Self meets true self in the context of how they may benefit one another, authentic communication takes place and we find, at least for a moment, that we have touched the soul of another, and through the other we have touched God.

For more information on classes, sessions, consultations, or newsletter call Gina Palmer, Animal Communications Consultant, or business manager Kim Patrick at the above number.

Parker, Alice Anne
Hau'ula, Hawaii
(808) 293-5833

Psychic • Reiki Master Teacher

Identified by *Honolulu Magazine* as one of Hawaii's best-known psychics, Alice Anne Parker is also recognized throughout the world for her work on dreams. She is the author of the bestselling *Understand Your Dreams,* and of the new metaphysical adventure novel based on the legendary Temiar-Senoi people of central Malaysia, *The Last of the Dream People.*

Alice Ann produced and hosted "Dreamline," a live, call-in radio show on dreams in Honolulu for five years. She has also written a regular feature on dreams for *Body Mind Spirit Magazine.*

Alice Anne is a Phi Beta Kappa graduate from Hunter College in New York City and holds a Masters Degree from Columbia University. She is an award-winning filmmaker, whose seven short films have been honored at the Cannes Film Festival, the New York Film Festival, the Venice Bienalle, and at a one-person show at the Whitney Museum of American Art. Her recent activities include work at Gregory House, a residential facility for AIDS patients, and volunteer work with inmates at Halawa Prison, a maximum security facility in Honolulu where she presented an ongoing dream workshop.

Alice Ann is an 8th generation Reiki Master Teacher. From 1973 to 1976 she trained with Dr. Thomas Maughan, Chief of the Ancient Order of Druids, in Great Britain.

Since 1973 Alice Anne has made frequent visits to Portland, where she offers residential dream workshops and Reiki Intensives. She is also available for psychic readings by phone. These taped sessions cover lifetime issues, focusing on areas of lifetime goals and mission — in addition to information on relationships, career choices, health concerns and opportunities for greater fulfillment in life.

For information on Alice Anne's future programs in Portland, please phone Lori Fletcher at (503) 281-2741. For information on readings or to schedule a reading by phone please call (808) 293-5833.

Alice Anne currently resides in Hau'ula, Hawaii, where she offers residential workshops and Reiki Healing Intensives at her home, a former Tibetan Buddhist Retreat Center. She continues her practice of psychic counsel to a world-wide clientele in the U.S., Canada, Great Britain, Germany, Greece and Switzerland. She can be reached at Buddha-Buddha, 53-086 Halai Road, Hau'ula, HI 96717. Please include a self-addressed stamped envelope for reply.

Parrott, Lexi, MA, Certified
Clinical Hypnotherapist
Portland, Oregon
287-4286 (w)

Hypnotherapist • Past Life Regression

We are beings of light, capable of great power, but we are trapped in identifies and projections that do not reflect who we really are. Our task is to free ourselves from the limitations, constraints, identities, and behaviors that keep us in lives that are unfulfilling, mundane, unhappy, and soulless.

Transformational hypnotherapy allows us to access power, release blocks, and reclaim our authentic self.

When we move to that deep level of relaxation we are able to access the source and solution of our problems and resolve them. This work is simple and effective. We create an energetic shift and our inner landscape changes, creating the space and opportunity for our lives to unfold in a new way. Sometimes this involves accessing our guides; sometimes it involves visiting past lives.

I received my Masters Degree from Berkeley and have studied with world masters in hypnotherapy. I have been involved in this work for many years and am in awe of its ability to transform and shift lives. It is an honor to partner with you in your sacred journey.

(*) Pauley, Rita
Lake Oswego, Oregon
(503) 636-3376

Psychic • Channeler

Rita Pauley uses her intuitive abilities to channel her guides during your session. She suggests that her clients prepare for a reading by writing down questions that are open-ended and request perspective, rather than predictions. For example, "I keep running into the same problem with my romantic relationships; what's your perspective on that?" Typically, the focus of the reading is on the client's present situation; information about the past and future may be brought in, as well. Clients benefit by gaining a new perspective on their lives that will help them on their spiritual path.

Peelen, Mary, M. Div.
Oakland, California
(510) 601-8963
E-mail: ohMary@msn.com

Psychic

I am a clairvoyant who does personal, in-depth, psychic readings. My readings focus on emotional, relational, spiritual, career, and health issues. I help clients see how past lives affect their present situations, and explore the future to help them make the best possible decisions. I also specialize in cleansing houses of negative energy. I work to release lost spirits and negative forces that are stuck in a home, replacing them with vital, joyful energy. I received a Masters of Divinity from the Graduate Theological Union in Berkeley, California, and I was trained in shamanic and other traditional techniques by Bethany Dalton. References available upon request.

Pennicooke, Mary
Portland, Oregon
(503) 232-7432

Healer • Reiki

Mary Pennicooke was born and raised in Portland, Oregon. She has lived and traveled world wide but Portland will always be home. Working in the service of others has been Mary's life focus. Being a paramedic for over 12 years and a firefighter for the last 7 years, adds to the overall total of more than 20 years of working in various traditional medical practices.

Her belief and practice of non-traditional therapies has been present most of her life. But her focused path in this area started in 1993 when she took a trip to Egypt with like-minded practitioners. Since then, she has begun her studies with Barbara Brennen at her school of intuitive healing sciences on the east coast. She also has earned the certification of Reiki Master.

Mary's approach to healing is holistic, working with her clients as complex, dynamic and unique beings. Healing occurs from within one's self, and Mary serves as a facilitator in this process. Each session is individualized for her client. Using techniques learned from Barbara Brennen, Reiki and information from her clients, Mary is able to receive guidance and works with her clients to bring them back to wholeness, back to their divine essence of who they really are.

Life naturally creates many traumas for us to learn from and overcome. These experiences are held within the body, creating blocks in energy flow. These traumas often happen in childhood and our belief system around that trauma is reinforced as we grow older. The healing techniques Mary uses will clear, balance and charge your energy fields, remove blocks that lead to dis-ease and enhance your body's natural healing potential. She may discuss various areas that influence your state of well-being, such as your health history, belief systems, your family and childhood history, diet, exercise and about you in relationships.

Mary has successfully practiced these techniques over long distances. It is not necessary to be physically present for a healing session, as we are composed of energy and consciousness.

Mary is willing and encourages working with a client's other healing practitioners. This process works in harmony with other types of therapy, including traditional medicine.

Your choice to find your truth, health and wholeness will not only affect your life, but also affect those around you.

We are all worth it.

Peterson, Bonnie
Brewster, New York
(914) 278-4352

Psychic • Astrologer

Bonnie Peterson is a psychic astrologer known nation-wide as one of the most powerful and accurate astrologers of this century. Her specialties consist of in-depth relation-ship compatibilities and health, legal, career and financial matters. Her celebrity predictions and horoscopes have been published in magazines and newsletters nationwide. Bonnie's reputation both as an incredibly powerful psychic and as a master of astrology has led to astounding improve-ments in the lives of every single one of her clients.

Bonnie began studying astrology over 20 years ago and recognized her psychic abilities at a very young age. She has predicted countless marriages, divorces, financial gains and health issues over the years for celebrities and laymen alike and has since devoted her life and career to guiding and advising people in nearly every area of their lives. Bonnie's unparalleled reputation in her field continues to strengthen even among psychics themselves.

After speaking with Bonnie you can expect to better understand your partner and your relationship. Bonnie will let you know if your relationship will be long or short term. She can give you the best dates for important events, chance encounters, financial gains and any health or legal issues you should be aware of. It is Bonnie's belief that we have a choice — to be masters of our fate or victims. Bonnie will help guide you to your personal destiny and fulfillment. Call 1-914-278-4352 for telephone readings by appointment or send written requests to Bonnie Peterson, RR3, Brewster, NY 10509.

Petroni, Nina Catherine
Newport, Oregon
(541) 574-6802

Clairvoyant • Tarot • Numerology

Nina's psychic talent emerged at the age of 7, when she had premonitions which subsequently turned out to be factual.

At the age of 19, she began a career in nursing terminally ill patients; with the aid of her clairvoyant abilities, Nina was proficient in determining her patient needs and became a spiritual healer.

Nina's achievements also include working as a youth counselor, helping guide troubled youths to a more fulfilling path.

Nina's talents include the abilities to perceive a person's future by holding an article belonging to them. When physically near a person, she can perceive a great deal about their past, present and future.

Nina has also communicated with the afterlife.

Nina began working with the Psychic Reader's Network (PRN) as a full-time psychic in 1994 because she felt it imperative to use her abilities to help others.

Nina is also a Tarot card reader and numerologist.

She feels like a guardian angel to people because she helps guide them to the light at the end of the tunnel. She enables them to see the opportunities life can offer.

Nina's satisfaction comes from helping others achieve more in their lives.

In addition to giving readings for the Guiding Light (PRN) and private readings, Nina recently wrote celebrity predictions for PRN's newsletter, the *Circle of Light*. She continues to write predictions for the newsletter, and she is organizing a psychic cruise.

Nina's future goals are to continue her work and assist in creating a new platform for psychic readers world-wide in the coming millennium.

Pietrokowsky, Faye, M.S.
Inner Design
Crystal Ball Productions
ide@transport.com
www.transport.com/^ide.
Fax: (503) 402-1096
Portland, Oregon
Phone: (503) 221-2123

Psychic • Teacher

Faye Pietrokowsky, MS, has two businesses in which she actively uses intuition as the basis of the services that she offers to private and corporate America. They are Inner Design and Crystal Ball Productions.

Inner Design is a service that helps individuals and corporations learn to use intuitive skills to increase productivity levels through enhanced decision-making and by increasing sales. Faye offers corporate intuition training seminars and coaches individuals to assist clients in achieving business goals. She also speaks to business organizations and associations on the subject of using intuition in the workplace ("How To Make Money Using Intuition" and "The Hunch That Got Away"). In addition she offers personal and business psychic readings, and often helps clients look at the available options to solving challenges.

Crystal Ball Productions is a fun fortunetelling party/event service that is available to corporations and people who want to offer clients, employees, and/or friends a unique form of entertainment. Faye dresses up in a gypsy costume and uses props, which include candles, cobweb, a

crystal ball, and glitter, and offers mini-readings to those
attending the event.

Pino, Carol
Hillsboro, Oregon
(503) 640-8687

Psychic

I am basically an energy mechanic. If you have a problem in a certain area, or if certain situations reoccur frequently, chances are strong that a habitual, reactive response keeps bring you to the same point. My job is to put you on my mental screen and locate the glitches.

Familiarity with several traditions enables me to find creative solutions to help you come to a point of assuming an active stance in your life rather than a reactive one. As a strong empath, finding energy patterns which are toxic to their creator is easy for me; however, each individual must assume personal accountability for their own actions and freedom.

As an experienced past-life tour guide, I enable you to discover which talents and experiences can enrich your life now, which need to be released, and how you can best utilize what you already know.

If you enjoy the uses of "stuff" in your spiritual practice, I can help you create your own altar, medicine pouch or other devotional focal point. A personal sacred place is greatly empowering and comforting.

I take clients if a conversation indicates it will be a

viable interaction. I can be reached at the telephone number above, and appointments will be scheduled during the day or early evening.

Platt, Mary
Portland, Oregon
(503) 245-7300

Psychic • Teacher • Healer • Reiki

My psychic ability has developed since childhood from a scatter of puzzle pieces. Dreams, out-of-body experiences, voices and visions provoked an intense interest in the world I sensed just beyond the physical. I never considered myself a psychic because I seldom "saw" the "future." My childhood dreams, however, were an important source of guidance, a window into worlds beyond my Oregon dairy farm. As a 10 year old, I felt strongly guided during an out-of-body experience that linked me with my adult self. Unlike most out-of-body experiences resulting from trauma, mine occurred on a quiet Sunday afternoon watching my family play a game. For a moment I was an adult, happy and confident, watching and appreciating myself as a child. That experience touched me deeply, helping to draw me through the pain and confusion of adolescence with confidence. Years later, during a time of profound hopelessness, I was "visited" by the elderly version of myself. Once again the experience was deeply touching and filled with specific guidance.

As a college student I studied Carl Jung and a variety of mystical traditions, searching for my psychic identity. In my late 20's my formal psychic training began. Initially attuned to Reiki healing by Mrs. Hawayo Takata, I have continued that practice, receiving my 10th generation Reiki Master Teacher degree from Alice Anne Parker. Also late in my 20's I explored channeling until I discovered that my interest lay in guiding other people through their own inner experiences. The material they encountered was always perfectly suited to their readiness to accept it. Process Work, an outgrowth of Carl Jung's work, has been a powerful influence. I value the close attention to the organic unfolding of experience with a minimum of dogma or technique.

The guided meditation process I use follows the structure of the chakra system; the "energy departments" of: physical vitality and resources/sexuality and creativity/ emotions/personal will/love and compassion/communica- tion/extended perceptions/ and the gateway beyond the personality outside of time and space.

The session lasts about an hour, beginning with a physical and mental relaxation. You and I establish the intention of mutual compassion and truth, linking with the earth and celestial forces. Your attention will be guided through the "energy departments" to clear and open their potential. You will be coached to maintain a deeply kines- thetic quality of attention that is rich and potent, strength- ening your subtle focus. The process of relaxation and subtle guided focus through the chakras creates a very deep conscious state that allows you to easily step out of time and space. Once in that expanded state I will guide you to expe- rience information, healing or guidance depending on your interest and needs.

The process is collaborative. During the experience we both share our perceptions and experiences in this deep inner state, testing the material against your sense of "rightness." I will encourage you to probe as deeply as you desire.

I take great care in creating a bridge between your inner experience and your current body, mind, emotions and spirit. All of my clients are visibly moved, renewed and refreshed after this inner journey beyond their personality. The state of limitless wholeness is deeply nourishing.

Some clients visit this "soul oasis" sporadically, while others wish to develop their intuitive skills with a personalized training series of three to five sessions.

Pope, Raphaela
Davis, California
(530) 758-6111

Telepathic Animal Communicator

From my earliest memories I loved animals. I used to embarrass my sister when walking down the street then by pretending to be a horse, prancing along, making clopping noises, and tossing my mane. As a child I fantasized that I had a Noah's Ark of animal buddies including cats, dogs, horses, birds, and bunnies. Now in my adult life, I get to actually live out this dream. I became a nurse, and worked for many years in critical care and rehabilitation. Simultaneously, I took workshops with my teacher, Penelope Smith, and began to develop my telepathic abilities. Gradually, over the years, my telepathic business grew, and I worked as a nurse part time. Finally, in 1996, I quit nursing altogether to devote myself full time to animal communication.

In my work as an animal communicator I talk to all kinds of animals and their people, usually about behavior and health issues. Why does my horse always blow up at this particular fence but not another one? What kind of treatment does my 12-year-old Persian kitty want for her mast cell tumors? Does Casey (dog) feel the acupuncture and Reiki treatments are helping his arthritis? How can I help Psycho-Kitty (real name) overcome her scratching and clawing habit? (Hint: change her name!) Does my aged bunny still want to stick around, or is he ready to leave his body? These are typical questions that people ask about their animal buddies.

I tune into the animal, hear their views and opinions on the situation, and communicate them to their people. Together we come up with strategies or changes acceptable to all parties. The animal is usually thrilled to be able to express herself, and sometimes the behavior changes immediately. One client told me a year after our consultation that when I asked Elmo (bunny) not to pee on the bed ". . . it was like turning off a faucet. He never did it again."

Rakitchenkov, Liza
Shamanic Energy Work
Berkeley, CA
(510) 869-4411

I am a healer in the shamanic tradition taught by Bethany Dalton-Kash. The force of this healing comes from the higher spiritual planes and from spirit guides and angels. This is an esoteric understanding and a deeply spiritual form of work. The healings are felt as gentle and loving connections to those divine forces. There is no touch involved in this therapy as you will be completely aligned and balanced by angels and guides.

The healings may be conducted over the phone. During my work I will see many things and I will talk about what's going on and explain the process. You will feel what is happening yourself even though there is no physical contact. A session lasts one hour.

Relief of symptoms due to stress or physical problems:

- Bone/tissue work
- Aura cleaning and healing
- Chakras balancing, cleansing and healing
- Increase joy
- Magnetic healing, vibrational healing with light

- Cleaning of various physical systems with divine Light
- Alignment with diving self or soul and body
- Removal of blockages: spiritual/mental/physical
- Cleansing/Purification/Rejuvenation
- Stimulation/balancing of organs and related systems

Working with all stages of pregnancy; mother-child connection and well-being

Randall, Penelope
Circle One
Woodland Hills, California
(818) 340-3550

Shaman

Penelope has trained with the Foundation of Shamanic Studies as well as with individual shamans and metaphysical teachers. Helping people to be all they were created to be is Penelope's goal in her shamanic work. Assisting people in their individual journey back to a whole, healthy, happy life is the core of her work in shamanic healing. Teaching the tools for helping people heal themselves can include the performance of the ritual known as soul retrieval.

The soul retrieval is an integral part of shamanic healing. Through trauma or injury a person may lose a piece of that vital life force we call the soul. This loss is a defense mechanism of the soul. The pain would be even greater if the person stayed whole during the trauma. In shamanic belief this part goes into another reality, often waiting for the call to come back. In modern psychology this fragmentation is known as disassociation; there is acceptance and an acknowledgment of the loss, but there is no effort made to bring the pieces back. The ritual the shamanic healer performs to bring these pieces back and restoring them to the person is known as Soul Retrieval.

Through the ritual of soul retrieval a person will experience a sense of wholeness and integration of self. Remembering the trauma associated with the original soul loss is not required in shamanic healing. Only the reintegration and the honoring of the return of those pieces is necessary for healing. The shamanic healer journeys into non-ordinary reality and finds any soul pieces that want to be helpful and wish to come home. Upon return to ordinary reality the shaman blows the found soul pieces back into the person's heart and the top of their head.

Penelope travels between Los Angeles and the Pacific Northwest. Her home base is in Woodland Hills, California, and she can be reached at the above number. She schedules appointments in the Pacific Northwest several times a year.

Reynolds, LaMoyne
Metamorphosis
Tigard, Oregon
(503) 244-1277
lamoyne@snsaccess.com

*Spiritual • Psychic Healings • Omega Energy Work •
Channeled Chats*

What Happens in a Session? Sessions are held at the
Metamorphosis office, and may be all healing energy work,
or all channeled information, or the always popular half and
half.

You keep your clothes on and relax either on a
massage table or in a chair.

LaMoyne places her hands on or near various parts of
your body. (Touch is not necessary, if it makes you uncom-
fortable.) Clients report the energy from her hands feels
warm or hot.

During the session, LaMoyne picks up information
stored in your body and shares insights given by the guides.
She works closely with her spirit doctor, Silverah; and her
wise and silly consultant, Ari. Occasionally other friends
and guides are present.

Omega Energy Work? Omega is a large, loving, trans-
forming hands-on healing method. It's very warm and
relaxing and comforting. It does not, however, tip-toe

around. If you're ready for change, or if you have a physical complaint, an Omega treatment can gently, yet powerfully, accelerate personal growth and self healing.

Call Metamorphosis for more detailed information about Omega; the benefits, where it comes from, how you can do it, too.

Pattern Pulling? Sometimes, the personal laws, memories, stresses, and injuries from this life (and other lifetimes) are stored in different parts of the body. Pattern Pulling, an Omega Light-Energy tool, allows us to energetically remove this extra baggage.

Moving Something Big? How About a Series of Sessions? If you're deep in the transformation process, a series of sessions can be very beneficial.

Psychic Circles. For the last couple years, LaMoyne has been offering Psychic Circles to introduce people to her work with Ari and Silverah, her Friends in Spirit.

At these gatherings, LaMoyne and her guides give their insights and opinions on relationships, health, family, work, and sometimes past life stuff.

LaMoyne's Healing Background. LaMoyne received attunements for several degrees from the Omega Shakti energy system, (including Electric Fire, Extasis, Magnetic Healing, and QMR - Quantum Molecular Regeneration) She has been involved in Body Harmony, and Re-Birthing, studied psychic and spiritual healing with Joseph Martinez and Bethany Dalton, and has a second degree in Reiki. She's a mom and also does technical writing and three-dimensional drafting.

Richards, Devin, LMT
Opening to Life
Portland, Oregon
(503) 299-4050

Psychic • Licensed Massage Therapist

Though I was very sensitive, empathic and kinesthetic as a child, my greatest openings and awakenings came with two near-death experiences in my late teens and early 20's (over 25 years ago). I began my spiritual practices with meditation and studied with numerous teachers.

Using a synergistic combination of ancient Eastern wisdom and Western healing concepts, my focus is to assist in awakening and releasing the transformative power within to heal all aspects of one's self. Moving through the physical, emotional, and subtle bodies, I sense and feel old holding patterns and blockages. I then use a wide variety of body and breath releases to clear and open the way for the flow of your life force and healing energies.

I enjoy creating an environment and opportunity for you to relax, to let go of tension and pain, and to open to receive more than ever before. To open to the breath, to the life force, to the healing and creative energies, to feel more freedom and flexibility, to feel more at home in your body and environment, to feel greater ease in giving and receiving, to fully connect with your own inner strength, wisdom and creativity.

For over 25 years I have continuously researched and explored leading edges of science, medicine, and Spirit for catalysts in natural healing and for creative expression. In sessions, I draw upon extensive training, personal and professional experience and intuition. I have worked in private practice for over 15 years and in conjunction with other professionals — osteopathic, chiropractic, and naturopathic physicians, psychotherapists, and other natural healers.

My education includes a Bachelor of Science degree in Allied Health Services and Education; license for massage therapy in the state of Oregon; certification in Cranial Sacral therapy; vast training in the field of natural vibrational healing and remedies, and a license as an ordained minister.

I would love to have the opportunity to share my work with you and to grow together. Blessings.

Roadman, Marilyn
Astrological Counseling Arts
Troutdale, Oregon
(503) 618-0800
marilyn@teleport.com

Astrological Interpretation and Counseling

"The story of any one drop, in the Ocean of Being, can be read in the synchronistic constellation of elements, manifesting throughout the cosmos." — Thom Fortson

I have studied astrology for 20 years and feel that it should be accessible to everyone. My entire life has been involved in the study of astrology, spiritual wisdom and helping/healing those who seek new insights, a greater understanding of themselves, and their own lives.

Life in today's sped-up world can be complex and confusing. Are you currently bewildered because the path ahead of you is a maze instead of a freeway? Are you faced with too many choices, too many risks, too many obstacles? Which way should you — can you — turn?

Would you welcome a road map?

Astrology is a reflective tool, just such a road map, to help us meet life's challenges with knowledge and spiritual awareness and to probe the unexplored territory in the depths of ourselves.

A private consultation includes natal chart, transit and progression study, plus yearly solar and lunar return charts. Ongoing and return consultations are also available.

Other services available include:

- Relationship Comparison (requires analysis of both natal charts)
- Astro-Carto-Graphy ™ Map(s) and Report(s)
- Unique "Pictorial Interpretation" of natal chart. Artistic, hand-drawn natal charts are colorful designs suitable for framing.

Reports:

- Personal Profile
- Relationship Analysis
- Transits and Progression Report
- Astro-Carto-Graphy ™ location and relocation influences
- Solar and Lunar Return Packages
- Past Life Insight
- Horang Quest Report — question or event based.

I am also a Cell Tech Distributor, Super Blue Green Algae: 1-800-269-9570.

May peace of mind and spirit always surround you!

Ryan, Jeri
Assisi International Animal Institute
P. O. Box 10166
Oakland, CA 94610-0166
Phone: 510-569-6123
Fax: 510-635-2351
E-mail: jryanimal@aol.com

Animal Communication

Hello. I'm Jeri Ryan. I am glad to set an appointment for you, and answer any questions. First, let me explain the routine. Once the appointment has been set, you might want to think of questions and issues that you want to talk about with your animal(s). Having these at hand can speed up the consultation. So you can fax or e-mail them to me ahead of time, or give them to me when we have the appointment.

At the time of the appointment, I will call you, and you can call me right back. That's because of the nature of the business: I aim to be on time, but it doesn't always work; something urgent might happen on the call prior to yours and I could be delayed. I don't want you to worry, however. Your name will be in my appointment book, so I will not forget you. If you have one or two animals and a few questions each, we can easily do that in one half hour. If you have several animals, and/or several questions, or if it could get complex, it is best to schedule an hour. If we run out of time, I will find another slot for you. I like to give my clients a financial break, so I treat the second appointment as though it was part of the first, so you can come out ahead financially.

I take emergency calls. Most common for me are medical emergencies. Others include questions about euthanasia, animals in pain, requests from veterinarians about health issues, dog-aggression, people-aggression, separation anxiety, depression, etc. If you have an emergency, please let me know its nature, and how late I can call you. For emergencies, I sometimes have to call late, and I am willing to do so. I communicate with all species of animals, since every living being has a spirit which makes it possible to communicate. My training and experience as a psychologist/psychotherapist prepare me to work with every kind of problem. Since I am not a veterinarian, I do not diagnose or prescribe. However, the animals can give us information about how they feel, and what they think is going on. That information can be useful to your veterinarian.

The animals have their own spiritual purposes, philosophical perspectives, and often quite a beautiful wisdom, and sense of humor. Our consultations often reach quite an emotional and spiritual depth, and can be such fun! The animals are amazing teachers!

As a Reiki Master, I can do third level Reiki healings, as well as energy/chakra healings, soul retrievals, past life regressions, and I am beginning to do hypnosis with nonhuman animals to assist them in healing themselves. These healings are not a substitute for medical treatment. They can enhance it, and have been known to heal independently. I also teach; i.e., I help people discover and develop their innate ability to communicate with animals, because, you see, everyone can do this. I teach all over the United States, and outside as well. If you are interested in organizing a workshop, please let us know. The organizer gets it free! I also lead workshops in Reiki.

I have founded Assisi International Animal Institute. We are nonprofit, and dedicated to education and rehabilitation. The education tracks include a certification program for people who want to become professional animal communicators, and one for people who want to learn to communicate for personal reasons. The rehabilitation track is for animals who ordinarily are euthanized for severe behavior problems. If you want more information, or would like to set up an appointment, or want to sponsor a workshop, please contact us using any of the phone numbers or addresses listed above.

Sarnia
Portland, Oregon
(503) 238-7225

Visionary Soul Portraits

While having a Soul Reading a beautiful "Visionary Soul Portrait" is formed through receiving energy, vibration and mental imagery. I use information surrounding your zodiac sign as well as using an oracle to help clarify your soul's purpose and personal path of evolution.

I gather specific information while sitting with you, such as: your favorite colors, important guides or totems, animals and any special connections you have with nature.

Before transferring a composition onto paper, I sit in meditation, to first recall our time spent together in our reading, and then to allow any further information to come through. If any important questions arise, I will contact you before proceeding with your "Visionary Soul Portrait".

Included with your soul portrait are two laminated copies, one approximately 8" x 11" and the second approximately 5" x 7", a good size you can carry in most daily planners. There will be a special card enclosed giving a detailed personal description of all the characters and symbols presented in your portrait. Also an example of your own personal greeting card is included.

You can choose to have a photograph taken of your soul portrait before framing, so you can continually create new ways to use and apply your "Visionary Soul Portrait".

I usually allow two weeks for completion. Prices of "Visionary Soul Portraits" vary according to size and detail. References available upon request.

Shore, Jon
13652 Shiloh Drive
Conifer, CO 80433
(303) 816-9247
budanatr@ix.netcom.com.
http://www.jonshore.com

Empath • Therapist

Ever since I can remember, I could feel, in my body and emotions, the feelings of those around me. When I was young, I could not discern between "my" feelings and those of someone else. I also had no idea that everyone could not do this. In college I began to realize that some people did not have the same empathic abilities I had. It wasn't until years later, as a therapist, that I realized that most people could not feel the feelings of others with the depth and accuracy that I could. I considered this ability more of a curse than a blessing most times. Although I couldn't imagine surviving without it. As the years went on and I became more Self-aware, I was finally able to discern between "my" feelings and others'. I still could not "turn off" the empathy, but it was a bit more in control.

In 1992, it was suggested by a friend that people could benefit from having their deep inner feelings "read." I wasn't sure this was quite true, but I was willing to use my abilities too help in any way I could. Reading someone to

the very center of their being, to the center of their Soul, is
very easy for me. I have always been 100 percent accurate.
It's as simple as touching water and saying, "This is wet."
If the reading were all that occurred, it would be very inter-
esting and possibly helpful in some ways. But I have
noticed that something else occurs during and after a
reading. With about eight out of ten people, it feels as if a
"switch" gets flipped on during the reading. When this
happens I know that their life is going to change, sometimes
drastically. It feels as if the "Hand of God" reaches through
me and touches their heart, their deep inner core, and
nothing is ever the same. The changes may be disconcerting
at first; but they have always ended up being good. I do not
take any credit for this happening, I am as much a witness
as the person I read.

I can feel and see all the light and all the shadows in
an individual. I can feel all the blocks and all the needs. In
the Soul, I can feel the sense of purpose. I can teach anyone
how to dissolve those blocks and shadows and how to live
a fulfilling and purposeful life. I also seem to be able to take
on some of the pain, depression, sadness, fear or anger of
the person I am working with. This gives them relief for a
few days or even weeks. They must keep these shadows
dissolved after that, using the practices I teach them. I can
help anyone find and feel that deep inner peace and joy that
is within them.

I am not a psychic. I cannot tell the future or the past.
But I can tell, with absolute accuracy, conviction and
honesty, what someone is and feels inside to the very core
of their being. I may or may not be able to discern the
source or situation that the feeling relates to, but I can
always see/feel the emotion. I can feel thoughts. I can
discern whether someone is being honest with themselves.

Time or distance doesn't seem to matter. I can do this process on the phone. I can also usually "read" someone that is emotionally connected to the individual I am talking with without ever meeting that distant person.

None of this seems very strange or unusual to me. I have been doing it all my life to one extent or another. I realize though that all of this may seem a little difficult to believe or comprehend to some people. I am always available and open to clarifying this work to anyone genuinely interested in it. It is my joy to do this work and, at this point in my life, I see my abilities as a great blessing to all who come to work with me and for myself.

It has been my experience and the experience of many others that this is a very powerful, life-changing session. Therefore, it should be entered into only by choice.

Simon, Lorena
Renton, WA 98058
(800) 821-5673 or
(206) 227-4289

*Clairvoyant • Clairsentient • Clairaudient •
Psychometrist • Natural Medium • Spiritual
Counseling • Healer • Telepathic Receiver.*

Lorena was born in Walla Walla, Washington, and has
lived most of her life right here in this state. Lorena was
born with her gifts and it runs in the family. She has been
developing and teaching others her very special talents.

A loving clairvoyant, God has bestowed this gift on
her to help any and all people who wish to enlighten themselves and bring a better balance into their lives.

Lorena helps people learn to protect themselves from
negative influences within and around them and stay
positive and manifest positive results into their lives.

We all have untapped powers and talent within
ourselves. With the help and the right tools of knowledge,
we can build the ability to take control of our own lives and
destiny. It's okay to have control of our self power.

Clients of all types and from many locations consult
Lorena — business people, couples, teachers, ministers,
psychologists, doctors, lawyers. They come from all over

the United States, Canada, Australia, New Zealand and England.

The police have consulted Lorena, along with family members, for assistance in solving cases of missing persons and murders.

With her natural medium ability, she has released lost or trapped souls who have made people's lives miserable and disruptive.

Charitable events and public speaking are dynamic vehicles for this psychic.

Lorena is well known for her caring and warm personality, along with her infectious laugh. An honest and loving approach makes her highly sought after in her field. Lorena has appeared on many programs, both locally and nationwide.

Lorena is an accomplished public speaker and has participated in a variety of forums including workshops, seminars, women's conferences, stage shows and the like.

Tapes of radio and television broadcasts are available upon request.

Simon, Marian, M.A.
Dallas, Oregon
(503) 831-0158

Shaman • Tarot • Spiritual Counseling

Shamanism and the Healing Effects of Soul Retrieval: Shamanism has existed for at least 40,000 years. (Eliade, 1964; Harner, 1980). The word Shaman comes from the Tungus peoples, a central Siberian tribe which means "one who knows in an ecstatic manner." (Grim, 1983). It is a spiritual healing method that accesses immediate knowledge of the sacred. The shaman embarks on a soul journey which entails a visionary experience in non-ordinary reality. (Eliade, 1964; Peters, 1989). Healing occurs while the shaman is in a trance state. The spirits work through the shaman to determine an illness, interpret dreams and visions, guide the souls of the dead, restore harmony and recover lost souls. (Grim, 1983; Ingerman, 1991).

An important purpose of shamanism is to connect the spirit world and ordinary reality. Shamanism is founded on the animistic belief that all things in the world and the universe have souls, are alive, possess consciousness and are interconnected. Animism is a belief in spiritual beings, the belief that souls may exist apart from bodies and that the soul is the principal of life and health. (Random House College Dictionary, 1980). The shaman, knowing that all things created have a soul, also knows that it is possible to communicate with these other spiritual essences by journeying to them, breaking through the barriers of time and space. The shaman's soul returns with the power of the universe which is the strongest medicine to be found. (Horwitz, 1995).

I was initiated to shamanism four years ago when a power animal appeared in my dream. The dream was extremely powerful and otherworldly. When I awakened, I was overwhelmed and I knew my life would change. A few months later, I fell seriously ill for nearly a year. I was forced to search the meaning of my illness and I realized I needed to fully embrace the notion that all things in the universe are connected through spirit. Spirits exist, are compassionate and are available to us for healing and divination. I realized my purpose in life was to be a healer.

Power, soul and energy are defined as a vital life force. Shamanic cultures believe that all disease has its origin in a disturbed relationship with the supernatural. (Hultkrantz, 1992). Illness is the result of a loss of power, energy or soul. Something or someone takes away our energy. Soul loss occurs when a part of our vital life force becomes separated from us due to an emotional or physical trauma. A disassociation occurs; that is, a part of the soul leaves and resides in the spirit world when a situation becomes too painful to bear. Disassociation is a survival mechanism which allows us to live through the trauma. The shaman travels to non-ordinary reality to ask the spirits for a healing, and following their direction, will perform an extraction, give advice or retrieve a lost soul.

A soul retrieval is a sacred experience. It is not meant to be a quick fix, and often the information given from the spirits is metaphorical and symbolic, which means that it may take time to reflect on the meaning of the experience. I have recently completed a research paper on the long-term effects of soul retrieval for the Institute of Transpersonal Psychology. The most significant results from my study on soul retrieval are: Increased self-awareness, confidence and inner strength; feeling whole, reconnected and complete; a greater ability to resolve issues from the past; inspired to make life changes. As a part of the human condition, no matter how fortunate or well adjusted we are, we always have a hunger to know more. A soul retrieval is not only important for vitality and health, but also to realize our purpose and meaning in life. In doing so, we free ourselves from the ordinary sorrows and confusions of life and achieve aliveness, joy and certainty.

Eighteen years ago I began to search the meaning of life when I became a student at the Pacific Northwest College of Art in Portland, Oregon. I was an intuitive artist and became interested in the creative interpretation of symbols from looking at art, the Tarot and Jungian dreamwork. I have a spiritual counseling practice in Salem, Oregon, where I utilize the Tarot, dream interpretation and shamanic healing practices to access the spirit world and the inner worlds of the deep self to gain clarity, insight and guidance, so that each of us may realize the gifts we are meant to manifest.

References

- Eliade, M. (1964). Shamanism: Archaic techniques of ecstacy. Princeton, NJ: Princeton University Press.
- Grim, J.A. (1983). The shaman: Patterns of

Siberian and Ojibway healing. Norman, OK:
University of Oklahoma Press.

- Harner, M. (1980). The way of the shaman: A
  guide to power and healing. New York, NY: Harper
  and Row.
- Horwitz, J. (1995). Animism: Everyday magic,
  Sacred Hoop. 9, 6-10.
- Hultkrantz, A. (1992). Shamanic healing and ritual
  drama. New York: The Crossroad Publishing
  Company.
- Interman, S. (1991). Soul retrieval: Mending the
  fragmented self. New York: Harper San Francisco.
- Peters, L.G. (1989) Shamanism: Phenomenology
  of a spiritual discipline. Journal of Transpersonal
  Psychology. 21(1), 113-121.

Smith, Benjamin
Port Orchard, Washington
(360) 876-5025
fax: (360) 895-0214
e-mail: benjamin@iammall.com
website: WWW.iammall.com

Intuitive Consultant • Past Life Regressionist • Tarot

Tarot: Benjamin has been reading Tarot cards for over 20 years. He does not use the traditional meaning of the cards; he uses the Tarot cards to do a psychic reading, telling you what the cards say about you or your questions.

Past Life Regressions: Benjamin has regressed thousands of people individually or in group regressions during his popular "Adventures in Past Lives" workshops. He is featured in Brad Steiger's book *Returning From the Light*, a book on using your past to shape your future.

Intuitive Consultant: Benjamin can work with you via the telephone as an intuitive consultant, assisting you in finding the answers you need to hear.

Benjamin is the founder of the International Association of Metaphysicians.

Suze
(pronounced "Suzie")
Portland, Oregon
503-768-4669

Psychic • Empath • Healer • Spiritual Counselor • Tarot • Medium • Teacher • Reiki

I have had 26 years of study about the mysteries of the universe. This includes numerous religious systems, saints and healers, and inquiries into quantum physics and the healing arts. I am a Reiki Master. I have studied harmonic sound with Jonathon Goldman, Ancient Egyptian Huna, breath work, Exodus, Amanae, Tibetan Dzogchen Buddhism, Merkaba and Advanced Merkaba, acupressure, Transcendental Meditation, and many more seminars and classes. I have attended Wings personal growth seminars and done a nine-month psychic development course. I also attended the Tom Brown Week-Long Survival Course in New Jersey. Tom is an international writer of many wonderful books which teach Native American wisdom and its incredible sense of spirituality.

I am a "holder of the light" and the "patterns" and symbols of light" of the Divine superconsciousness. I work with a community of spirits, including the Angelic Master

of Sound (who is known as Shamma-El and Metatron),
Masters and Beings of Light of the higher creation, and the
energies of Power Without Form. There is so much
confusion, so much stress coming in from relationship
issues, from the job, from spiritual processes happening to
humanity, that people are trying to find where they really fit
in and find the balance within themselves. We can help
people to balance and be able to step out into the world in a
more powerful way. The session can be anything from a
profound and powerful initiation to a soft, gentle and
supporting one.

We wrap people in a gentle but powerful blanket of
light and help them feel secure and supported. In draw in
energy from the heavenly dimensions and from the earth,
and infuse a spirit of unfoldment within them. In my
deepest visionary state, I can pull in many aspects of heaven
and earth at the same time to help them unfold the uncom-
fortable truths of where they are in their life right now
without judgment. We show them how they got there and
the Greater Truth that wants to unfold within them. My
toning sets up harmonious vibrations that search out that
Truth and infuse the body in each chakra (each energy
center in the body) with a sense of support. At the same
time, this frees up the inharmonious energies directly from
the cellular structure and energy bodies. Each session
involves discussion and a spiritual reading. It brings mental
and emotional support, and an inner framework of energy,
activating and resonating each energy vortex in our body.
We create a capsule of energy around the person that helps
them to feel more open and receptive, yet protected at the
same time. It feels loving and nurturing so they can move
out more and more into the world and feel that strength
within them.

People become more in tune with their own nature and have clarity, light and truth. They find their own excitement and become aware of their own radiance and divinity. This can be a joyous experience, with laughter and love. Some have even seen and felt that "Seed of Light," that lightform of the Divine, who they really are. They break down in joyous tears of gratitude and remembrance of the Greater Reality. It is always a spontaneous thing that happens. Many of the people I have worked on have now become strong enough to be the teachers they came to earth to be. I offer a rich menu from which you can draw information and energy. Besides the groups listed below, we can also use various tools such as numerology, Mayan Oracle cards, your "Mayan imprint" (the energy when you were born), Tarot cards, crystals and stones to help you discover more.

Groups:

Introduction to Energy. Safe, special, supportive evenings provide a way for people to come together to open to the spiritual realms, to find out about and express their gifts. Education and experiences of the energy fields, the energy laws of thought, feeling and manifestation, and spiritual gifts.

Toning Work Using the Sacred Sounds, Cosmic Breath and Energy Core Dynamics. We create a structure, a field of energy that is drawing up from the earth and from the heavens in a balanced way. This creates a vibratory resonance as we open to our divine superconsciousness, to the Angelic Master of Sound, the realms and Beings of Light of the higher creation, and our own kundalini energies. We open to gain spiritual intelligence and connection, and to clear and balance our chakras and energy bodies. We create a powerful group energy that can be felt very noticeably spiraling through the group. We become messengers to bring upliftment to earth and humanity. During the circle, we direct the healing energies to ourselves, our loved ones, and the earth.

Group and Long-Distance Healings. We infuse others with heart energy and strength of spirit. We also do hands-on healing on each other.

Earth Grid Work. This is special work for bringing higher consciousness and healing in to earth. It rebalances negative energies in the mass consciousness of humanity. We provide assistance to Mother Earth in her birth process of bringing us the fourth/fifth dimensional reality. The Life and Teachings books say, "Call this fourth dimension or what you wish, we call it God in expressions, through the Christ in us." When the dimensional shift occurs, other-dimensional beings will be seen and heard by all humanity.

Personal tapes for relaxation and growth are available also. Experience soothing energies and voice toning specifically tuned to you. Centers the chakras, aligns and relaxes. It has the focus of personal empowerment — energizing and relaxing at the same time. Continues to open you to the higher consciousness. Feels as if you are being carried in a soft blanket of energy.

Swanepoel, Jenny
Portland, Oregon 97225
(503) 641-9167
e-mail: Jenny@coach2k.com
fax: (503) 641-1689

Personal Success Coach

Mentor/coach: a resource for Healers, Pathfinders and Wayshowers. "I do just about everything that I love, and I help my clients do the same."

The role of an athletic coach is well known. A personal coach fulfills the same function in the game of life! The coaching relationship is a privileged one, rooted in trust and mutual respect. It is a professional designed alliance, focusing on maximizing opportunity, not just on solving problems. A coach is a combination of counselor, consultant, best friend and cheerleader! She helps design an action plan and "stays with" the client to implement it, providing insight, accurate feedback and encouragement.

Psychics and healers have a particularly challenging role in the transformation of our society. Jenny offers support, stability and balance for these endeavors, as well as insight into marketing and professional/business development. She integrates both right- and left-brain wisdom, bringing professional training as a counselor, vast and varied life experience and a deep spiritual connection to the meeting.

For mutual convenience, she works mainly by phone and e-mail. Clients call in at a prescheduled time for an hour's tele-coaching, usually once a week for the time period required to achieve the desired outcome. She insists on two free sessions before accepting a paying client, as a comfortable "fit" is essential for the process.

(*) Teabo, Shirlee
Federal Way, Washington
(253) 839-6281

Tarot • Parapsychology Consultant

Shirlee is well known throughout the United States, Canada, and Mexico. A professional psychic for 28 years, she has appeared hundreds of times on radio and television in the U.S. and Canada, and has been the subject to numerous newspaper and magazine articles.

With her sister, Jacquie Witherrite, she co-authors a weekly newspaper column, "The Curious Psychic," that appears in Tacoma's *Morning News Tribune.* She is the author of *Evolution of a Psychic,* an autobiography. Humorous and compelling, her book explains why she believes there are no accidents; that everything occurs for a reason, and why caring souls are coming together to unlock new doors of awareness.

Shirlee also hosts a weekly television show, "Psychic Northwest." She has been featured in two of Ruth Montgomery's books: *Aliens Among Us* and *Threshold to Tomorrow.* She is also listed in *100 Top Psychics in America.*

Personal, private readings are scheduled in half-hour or one-hour sessions. The cards focus on personal issues such as money, relationships, job, and what is happening in the immediate future.

She lectures at colleges and universities on psychic phenomena and has assisted police in criminal investigation.

Thompson, Marie
Columbia, South Carolina
(803) 798-6699

Psychic

I discovered my psychic abilities when I was in my early forties. Until that time I had no explanation for many of my strange life events, such as making the highest score ever recorded on the Education GRE at the university where I got my masters degree. This was extraordinary because I had never had any undergraduate courses in education. Years later I understood this was a reflection of my psychic ability.

The presence and power of my psychic abilities became obvious while I was participating in a healing group led by a psychotherapist who was herself a psychic. She (Judy Johnson) performed her work through her intuitive gifts. I was fascinated by the fact that she maintained no records and took no notes yet knew everything about whichever individual she attended.

In this atmosphere of intense love, truth and heightened awareness, I discovered I was a clairsentient (one who connects to the psychic realms through their feelings and body sensations). Until that time I thought everyone had the same connection to the emotional realms. I was surprised to find out this wasn't so. Since this discovery, I have put a tremendous amount of energy into developing my gifts. The vehicle that best suits the expression of my talents is the Tarot. I have worked with many other methods of divination (numerology, card science, astrology) and I blend these powers into my Tarot readings.

When people come to me for a reading, they most frequently want to know about the future of relationships, finances, work and health. I tell them what I sense about the future and I also include what I call "the bigger picture." The bigger picture is the real meaning of the situations and people in my client's life. It speaks to the evolution of the soul through experience. In my work as a psychic I function as a bridge between the personality of my client and their Higher or God Self. Every situation that I am presented with I view through the eyes of the soul. I actually work with transmutation — converting the mundane into the sacred.

Anyone who comes to me for a reading can expect to come away with accurate information and concrete recommendations. They can also expect to feel better at the end of a reading with an expended vision of themselves and their process. Going from hopeless to hopeful always involves being able to see the Light at the end of the tunnel.

Tyler, Elizabeth Boyd, M.A.
Paths to Wellness
Lake Oswego, Oregon
(503) 699-8378

Intuitive Readings • Reiki • Counselor

Elizabeth Boyd Tyler holds a Masters Degree in Clinical Psychology with over 20 years' experience as a counselor, teacher and seminar leader. Elizabeth utilizes training in Psychosynthesis, T'Ai Chi, Qigong, Guided Imagery & Music Therapy and Pleiadian Lightwork in her uniquely integrative approach to healing and wellness. Elizabeth is also a Reiki Master and a Certified T'ai Chi Chih instructor.

Elizabeth's focus is on living in the vibration of the heart and the alignment of mind, body and spirit. She brings together a rich background of skills to design a healing program unique to your special needs. Elizabeth also does chakra clearing and balancing, along with intuitive readings to help you release beliefs and energy patterns that no longer serve you. You will leave a healing session feeling more connected to your heart and soul, along with having a bag of self-healing tools to help keep you on your path of empowerment and wholeness.

Vanderbeck, Philemon
Seattle, Washington
(206) 329-6929

Tarot • Runes • Dream Interpretation • Chocolate Readings

Philemon Vanderbeck was reincarnated on 30 August 1965 at 12:25 a.m. in Greenock, Scotland. He moved to the Pacific Northwest approximately 20 years ago and picked up his first Tarot deck around the same time. Since then, he has been helping people by revealing the hidden influences in their lives.

Tarot: Philemon considers himself to be an intuitive, and his favorite tool of choice is the Tarot. He approaches the art of divination from a psychological perspective and after beginning the reading by giving a general overview of the cards laid out, engages the querent through interactive questioning to clarify the situation and explore the possible strategies and solutions.

Runes: Philemon is also quite proficient at the art of Rune casting and interpretation. Deliberately ignoring certain recent publications that are unfortunately flawed in their information, Philemon instead uses the original methods and interpretations as developed 2000 years ago.

These techniques create a pattern that reveal the various flows of energy currently affecting the querent's present situation and sometimes reveal the affect specific decisions may have in creating alternate outcomes.

Dreams: Fascinated by dreams ever since he remembers having them, Philemon also helps others learn how to interpret their own dreams. Since the same symbol may mean quite unique things to different people, Philemon doesn't rely on dream dictionaries but uses a combination of modern interpretation techniques and interactive exploration to decipher the language of the subconscious found in the nocturnal landscape.

Chocolate Readings: An exclusive offering of Philemon's is his Chocolate Readings. This technique was designed primarily as an entertaining introduction to the realm of divination and symbol interpretation. By having the querent select a chocolate from an assorted box of Godiva truffles and while they consume it, have them describe the imagery that the exquisite confection invokes, Philemon is able to interpret the images to reveal hidden desires.

Philemon is a regular counselor and instructor at Astrology Et Al bookstore, and has appeared at the Boeing Psychic Fair, EndFest '97, Entros restaurant, Microsoft Company Picnic, and various other locations. He has also created special workshops on each of the above divination techniques for private home parties and corporate functions. You can reach him by calling the number above.

Vicino, Esther, U.C.M.
Albany, Oregon
(541) 967-3035

Psychic Counseling • Readings • Self-Improvement Classes

Esther Vicino is a world-traveled psychic and consultant to a world-famous rock star hall of famer, several actors and actresses. She has a following of clients across the United States who rely on her for telephone consultations and counseling. Her psychic work has brought her to help people in other parts of the world including France, Africa and Japan. Esther has been on numerous television and radio talk shows.

Esther has been actively practicing spiritual counseling since 1953, even before the dawn of the new age. Born with a unique vision, she has studied parapsychology in New York and California to fine-tune her talents. She became an ordained minister in 1986 with the Universal Church of the Master in Santa Clara, California.

Her work includes:
- Psychic consultations
- Spiritual counseling
- Phone readings nationally/world

- Self-improvement classes,
- Self-Esteem
- Positive Thinking
- Breaking unwanted habits
- Self-Healing Techniques
- Visionary Image Development
- Greater Use of Own Capacity
- Lost Articles Found
- Wedding ceremonies performed
- Workshops — Lectures
  Bonus for 5 referrals

Esther is a unique and caring soul. Let her help you to bring your inner spirit alive. Experience some of her original qualities and change your life forever.

Living life in stability and love is what Esther is all about.

(*) Vivian
Beaverton, Oregon
(503) 671-9041

*Spiritual Healer • Teacher • Psychic • Past Life
Regression • Tarot • Emotional Process Intuitive*

Understanding the complexities of the Universe may be overwhelming. Many people spend their entire life studying, experiencing and using Universal Power. Individuals who dedicate their lives to these studies are usually healers, teachers, or clergy. Some have developed "gifts of Spirit," others are learning these gifts, and some are exploring the possibilities. Each person will experience this Universal Energy for themselves and find their own truth and knowledge.

Vivian presents a personal development approach to spiritual skills. She believes that Spirit is asking us to use the energy in our own lives and experience the results through personal achievement (Bringing Spirit into Form). When building a foundation through personal experience we can radiate the results into the world as we expand, develop, and explore our unlimited potential.

Vivian focuses on the Spiritual aspects of healing while incorporating mental, physical and emotional well-being. By identifying and clearing the emotional and the mental levels you can begin to identify the needs of your spirit. Healing begins within the spirit.

Vivian offers several types of Personal Development Sessions.

Intuitive Counseling. Vivian can assist in identifying and eliminating trauma from the spirit so that you can achieve a sense of well-being and wholeness.

Holistic Coordination. Vivian can help you to understand the many forms of Holistic Therapies available, and assist you in coordinating a supportive, easy-to-use program. She works closely with many holistic practitioners and will guide you in setting up your own network of practitioners. Vivian can help you develop personal techniques that support your body, mind, emotions, and spiritual well-being.

Lifestyle Planning. By applying spiritual qualities to your everyday life you can inspire and encourage daily spiritual well-being. Vivian can teach you practical, down-to-earth methods for reaching your dreams.

Teaching.

- Tools & Techniques for Self Transformation
  "Bringing Spirit into Form"
- Spiritual Guidance and Insight Education
  To assist each person with a path to health and
  well-being.
- Personal Development for Conscious Living
  Individuals, Couples, Families.

Also available are workshops, lectures, home blessings, wedding consulting, and wedding ceremonies.

Warmoth, Ron
PO Box 4037
Los Angeles, CA 90078
(213) 389-3483

Dowser-Psychic • Clairaudient • Clairvoyant

Ron Warmoth is one of the most documented psychics currently practicing. He has established an impressive record of successes by using his psi-dowsing talents for personal and business counseling, locating oil, gold, water, and archaeological finds. He has been teaching and lecturing on parapsychology nearly 30 years, and is often seen on national television.

Recently, an NBC TV crew filmed a segment on-site showing Warmoth locating rare pink tourmalines. During the taping, Blue Sheppard, the owner of the mine, swung against the side of the rock tunnel where Warmoth indicated, until a large chunk of rock fell away. Picking up one of the rock pieces, the amazed miner said, "Right here in this spot where you psychically saw it — pink tourmaline." Another dozen blows opened a pocket of hot pink crystals. "Here it is," Sheppard explained, "in a place where it shouldn't have been!" This particular piece of footage is the only known nationally telecast segment showing dowsing being done on an actual project.

Warmoth's practice is international in scope. He has scored successes on-site in Chile, Mexico, Canada, Greece, Dominican Republic, Costa Rica, Southeast Asia, Alaska's north slope and Yukon regions, and sites across the lower 48 states. His abilities have been investigated and reported in Newsweek, Los Angeles Times, London Daily News, and over 600 other publications.

Warmoth expresses a philosophy that values the individual and has always been available to those with everyday problems of living — and has a listed phone number. He also writes a monthly letter, in its 18th year of print. The Ron Warmoth Letter is a psychic-metaphysical journal which provides ideas, examples, and specific directions designed to expand the reader's awareness of the law of mind and his or her unlimited self-potentials.

Wiley, Susan
Intuitive Consulting
Hillsboro, Oregon
(503) 640-2511

*Clairvoyant • Clairaudient • Empathic • Artist-sketch
your energy field • Angels and Guides • Past Lives •
Intuitive knowing • Channel for information • Energy
Readings • Energy Balancing*

Each person has a spiritual energy with a unique
expression of light. In reading your energy field, I employ
various intuitive abilities, I am a clairvoyant, empath, and
an energy intuitive. I can reach into a multidimensional
universe that is full and vibrant with information that may
assist you in your growth. Through visually accessing your
auric field, colors, imagery, and symbols open up to me.
Frequently, panoramic moving scenes appear. These can
give me a sense of where you are now in your life, parts of
your past, and occasionally past lives. I sense where your
energy is more fully and joyfully wanting to express itself.
Trained in Therapeutic Touch and other energy disciplines,
I can assist you in helping yourself to balance your energy
field. Sometimes angels and guides appear to assist with
information and guidance. Occasionally, I describe a loved
departed one that appears and can give details on the

personality, visual description, emotions, or other signature qualities. As an artist, I have been told I give unusually clear descriptions of anything I see. I can sketch your energy field in color, and any symbols that may want to appear with it. Each session can have a different focus, depending on the information I receive.

At age 18 I predicted a Pan Am plane crash I was to be in. The details I clairvoyantly received showed me I was to survive, and that it was important for my maturing to go through the experience. The crash itself offered many "growth" opportunities, but the awareness that I had seen many of the details ahead of time had the greater impact on my life. A seed for deeper spiritual understanding had been planted. From my experiences with the crash and many experiences since, I understand we are masters of our own life journey. There is a loving spiritual intelligence behind our seemingly chaotic choices. My gifts may bridge the gap to help awaken awareness within you.

Throughout the last ten years I have given readings to friends and clients, and have been involved in various intuitive growth groups. I have helped people open up some of their own intuitive nature, and I occasionally hold classes on intuitive development.

Working with your questions and concerns can be a creative and rich adventure as we draw from many dimensions. I have been told by various clients and intuitive groups that I offer information in a gentle and compassionate way. I experience great joy and passion in my work.

Day and evening appointments.

For more information, call between 10:00 a.m. to 8:00 p.m. weekdays.

Wolfer, Suzie, Rev., MSW
Earth School Institute
Portland, Oregon
(503) 224-3318
www.teleport.com/~swolf/earth-
school

Intuitive Readings. Do you find yourself at a cross-
roads? Low on energy or enthusiasm? Feel like you're
driving with your brakes on in life? Your life force may be
stuck. In our session together, you will meet your "higher
self" — the You that contains your body. You will glimpse
the blueprint of your life, where even difficult life experiences support your growth. Seeing the larger purpose in
challenges with relationships, money and health gives you
the power to make your own course corrections and create
breakthroughs to the life you really want. As you come to
understand your deeper reasons for being here, you begin to
see how the curriculum of your daily life serves this
purpose. A reading may help you move through the
crossroad, feel the wind in your sails again, and move
forward with renewed inspiration and energy.

Mediation. Have you ever thought of meditation as
fun? . . . Body Centered Meditation is a pleasurable way of
listening deeply to a profound wisdom inside of you. When
you focus inside, the whispers of your own wisdom rise up
like a melody on a warm afternoon breeze. Body Centered

Meditation tools help you embrace the body's reality without becoming lost in it, nor ignoring it. As you work in harmony with your body, you heal the split between body and mind. Finding well-being inside you frees up a fountain of peace, joy and creativity. As you calm the inner storms, you unleash the powers of genius, passion of mind and deep sense of purpose in your everyday life.

Breath work. Most of us breathe upside down. We actually hold tension in the body. Effective breathing dissolves depression, tension and pain. Breath connects us with our bodies and with the cosmos so we become fully alive and radiant again.

Body-Centered Psychotherapy. When you meet with me, I may use a variety of approaches including: Body-Centered Psychotherapy, Meditation, Intuitive information, Conscious Breathing and Classical Homeopathy. I've found that early in life most of us developed a split between body and mind. Messages from our bodies were ignored by our minds. Over time, this gap widened, making us distrust our bodies. This painful split shows up in our adult life in many ways:

- Troubling emotions like depression, anger, grief, shame or low self esteem
- Relationship problems
- Shallow breathing patterns
- Chronic health problems
- Addictions.

Untended, this gap widens, It demands relief through addictions such as food, alcohol, work, people, shopping or drugs. We attempt to feel good through artificial means. Sadly though, our well of pain deepens.

The "body-centered" approach that I use calls back into our well of pain. Feelings of isolation, grief and anger transform into feelings of belonging, celebration and aliveness. As we acknowledge and heal this split between body and mind, we open the door to our own wisdom again. Making this simple and powerful shift releases a deep current of creativity. And After a while, like the oak tree, it feels natural and wonderful to be magnificent.

Training and Classes. I am delighted to offer training in intuition development, meditation, healing, emotional intelligence and couples and family communication. I also enjoy performing weddings and other life passage rituals. Please call for more details or to make an appointment at the number above. Also check out my web page.

Wynn, Katrina, M.A.
Yachats, Oregon
(541) 547-5123 office
e-mail: katrina@igc.apc.org

Tarot • Counselor • Teacher

The study and teaching of the ancient metaphysical laws and lessons symbolized in the Tarot is my greatest passion. Tarot cards represent the sacred journey of our soul through this existence we call life. In reading the cards they reflect back to us the aspect of our journey that is unfolding in the moment and the potential energy and wisdom we may gain from the experience or challenge we are involved with. This approach goes far beyond mere fortune telling and predictions, touching us at our core, going to the heart of the matter. Thus, the Tarot is a model and method of transformation, that magical process through which we pass from the known, over the edge of our perception, to the great mystery.

My gift in working with clients using the Tarot is enhanced by years of experience as a psychotherapist, training in the healing arts, and my calling as a spiritual guide. I blend my intuition and knowledge with my client's energy to unfold the spirits at work and their lesson for us in the reading. Sometimes I feel like a spiritual midwife, helping new life to be born.

Call me to find out my annual Tarot Retreat in the woods.

In private practice in Yachats, Newport, and Portland for the past seven years with a compassionate, wise presence I help individuals, couples and/or groups explore various challenges and life experiences to support healing and growth. I have an eclectic approach in counseling with training and experience working with many unusual and meaningful aspects of life, including mediations and conflict resolution, cultural awareness and honoring diversity, Native American and other spiritual beliefs and lifestyles, women's issues, men's issues, sexual issues and politics, addictions, and metaphysics.

As a Universal Life Minister I am available to perform unique, creative, non-denominational ceremonies cele-brating birth, death, a rite of passage, or marriage/ bonding/handfasting.

Please call my toll-free line for appointments, private sessions, classes, to receive a Tarot newsletter or to be on my mailing list.

Education and Credentials:

- Doctor of Metaphysics
  Universal Life Church
- Master of Arts/Counseling Psychology
  Antioch University, Seattle, WA
- Bachelor of Arts/Community Studies
  UC Santa Cruz, CA
- Master Hypnotherapist
  Twin Lakes College, Santa Cruz, CA
- Natural Health Educator
  Twin Lakes College, Santa Cruz, CA

- Certified Massage Therapist
  Twin Lakes College, Santa Cruz, CA
- Universal Life Minister
  Universal Life Church, Modesto, CA

Currently completing certification in Process Oriented Psychology, Process Work Center of Portland with 10 years' training and experience.

Twenty-five years of Tarot and metaphysical studies, seven years experience teaching locally and abroad.

Teachers:

Tarot: Vicki Noble (Mother Peach); James Wanless (Voyager); Angeles Arrien (Thoth); Jamie Sams (Medicine Cards and Sacred Path); Amber Jayanti (Waite), Lady Dorothy (Albano-Waite).

Astrology: Demetra George (Asteroid Goddesses & Dark Moon Goddess); Jonathan Tenny (Motherpeace); Jim Lewis (Astrocartography), and Jeffrey Green (Soul & Pluto).

(*) Young, Allen David, Ph.D.
Aquarian Institute
Berkeley, California
1-800-592-2733

Psychic Counselor • I Ching • Astrology • Tarot

Allen David Young, Ph.D., has been doing psychic-based counseling, intuition training workshops, and organization development consulting since 1979. Much of his counseling work is done over the telephone. He is a Science of Mind Practitioner, author of the book *Vision & Change*, and audio tapes on intuition training and the I Ching.

He makes regular visits to Portland, Seattle and Vancouver, and reads at New Rennaissance Bookshop whenever he's in Portland.

Z, Dawna
Portland, Oregon
(503) 760-3113

***Intuitive Readings • Dreamwork • Touch Drawing
Workshops***

Intuitive Readings: While in a light, meditative state I see with my inner vision, the energy surrounding issues of health, relationships, career, lifepath and past lives. My particular focus is to bring you information to assist you in living a fulfilling, healthy life. I offer gentle non-invasive healing energy when it is desired and appropriate.

Dreamwork: May be done within an intuitive reading session or in a separate session. I use my intuition and dreamwork skills to assist you in deepening your understanding of the messages of your own unconscious wisdom.

Touch Drawing Workshops: A unique opportunity to directly access your soul's wisdom and creativity. In the technique of Touch Drawing, a sheet of paper is placed over a smooth surface of wet paint. Wherever the paper is touched an imprint is left on the underside. Impulses from within are released on the paper. Many drawings are created in one sitting, each flowing into the next, guiding one deeper into the self. The workshops are given in a safe supportive environment and may include meditation, movement, journaling and music.

Biography:
- Certified First Degree Reiki healer since 1993.
- Earth School Institute Intuitive Training Program graduate 1997.
- Studied dreamwork individually and in groups using the work of Jeremy Taylor as a framework since 1995.
- Studied Touch Drawing at the Center for Touch Drawing in Langley, Washington 1998.

Personal Statement:
I have successfully used my intuition to help guide my own life. It is my deepest desire to assist others in finding and following their own unique soul's voice.

(*) Zakara, Maki and Jared, M.A.
Portland, Oregon
(503) 284-8542

Psychics • Healers

A lot of beautiful work has been written about unconditional love, inner work, and forgiveness. Spiritually minded people work hard and diligently on these areas. But sometimes, though their efforts are admirable, they are unable to reach the level they would like to. We believe that what prevents them from reaching their highest vision is that they carry emotional hurt and suffering from the past. Everyone is walking wounded in varying degrees. It isn't always the devastating emotional trauma that severely wounds a person. Sometimes it is as subtle as going through years of feeling you couldn't be accepted as you are or being criticized by your family or partner. Part of being human and living life is being hurt, but so far it seems we haven't known how to heal the pain in ourselves.

As people grow up in childhood and get hurt in the process, they inevitably split from the pain because it is too overwhelming for them. By the time they reach adulthood they have several split-off parts that they are unaware of. The mental body, inner child, higher self, and other parts less defined are all competing under the mast of your personality. One part wants a certain job and another part isn't interested in that career at all, so the person is only marginally successful. Relationships often have difficulties when one part agrees to things while another part has unexpressed needs, feelings, and boundaries that then get acted out. Eventually the body reflects this imbalance in disease and chronic illness. Our work gently, but effectively, integrates all these parts and the person comes away with a new sense of wholeness and inner peace.

As you continue your journey to reconnect with yourself, forgiveness is crucial. It is the key that opens the door to the heart and the soul. Forgiveness is a concept that is often not fully understood. People always think this means simply to forgive those who have hurt us in the past. But it is just as essential to forgive yourself for all the times you have hurt others and separated from your true nature. This enables you to finally let go of all the guilt and regret you carry and learn to truly love yourself, but this cannot be fully done if a person is not integrated. One part wants to forgive while another is still hurt and bitter, then feeling guilty and undeserving of forgiveness themselves. Once we have helped someone integrate, we guide them through a forgiveness process that leads them back to themselves. Forgiveness, full circle, is the path to deeply sincere unconditional love.

What prevents the light and love of Spirit flowing through you is the emotional pain held from the past that blocks the heart. People work on overcoming their emotional past, but it is simply too painful to go through all the layers of many years. Over the past year we have developed short-term methods that clear all emotional suffering, imprints and karma in a gentle way, with the person feeling a mere 10 percent of the emotions as they pass through, usually in 10-12 sessions. The healing combines energy work, hypnosis, NLP, process work, past live regression, chakra cleansing, and strong channeled healing energy. This work is very powerful and will change every area of your life, your heart, and your soul. Experience: agelessness, perfect health, loving relationships, abundance, passion-filled life purpose, and ecstasy. Call for free telephone consultation.

Zimmerman, Adele
Kalispell, Montana
(406) 755-4905

Interspecies Communication Consultant • Teacher •
Certified Holographic Repatterning ™ Practitioner

My work incorporates the principles of honoring and appreciating all life. Every time I communicate with another being, including a person, I appreciate our mutual sharing, how we help each other grow, regardless of whether the interaction flows positively or is challenging, pushing our edge of acceptance and ease. I know that we are all One, mutually connected in love and equality. My personal goal is to live 100 percent in this knowing. I see myself serving this planet and all beings who live here, by fostering peace through communication, compassion, and understanding. Once someone understands another from the depths of one's heart, it is difficult, if not impossible, to fear or dislike the other. I used to struggle against the darkness, fighting against cruelty and injustice, but the "light bulb" has lit up in my life, and now I put my energies into spreading the light, focusing on what I am "for" rather than what I am "against."

My animal friends help me so much, modeling

innocence, joy, acceptance, and being in the moment. I believe that the awareness of my personal experiences helps me to approach my work in interspecies communication with compassion.

During a consultation we center ourselves on the unconditional love that radiates in and around us, in a way that feels so natural and easy. My approach is that the person and animal friend are in partnership, both having the best intentions based on where they are at the time. We work with whatever issues are of concern, moving to increased awareness, appreciation and agreement.

Having experienced and learned from the deaths of several close animal friends, I also offer grief support to animals and people and help them prepare for a parting when the animal is elderly or has a potentially terminal illness. My focus is on helping both beings deepen their bonds, knowing that the physical connection is very precious, and also that the connection transcends the physical and continues after death. My clients in grief counseling have been so relieved to know that they can communicate and continue their loving relationship beyond death. As a result of this understanding, their grieving process flows more quickly to healing, comfort and peace.

In addition to interspecies communication consultations, I provide Holographic Repatterning for people and their animal friends. A Holographic Repatterning session uses muscle checking and communication to bring into awareness the unconscious patterns and energy constrictions that are underlying one's specific problems and challenges. After identifying the issues, which is a healing process in itself, we move through the appropriate self-healing modalities to help restore the animal or person's energy to optimal frequencies for well-being.

Individual consultations are offered on-site (for local clients) and long-distance by phone. Communication consultations are scheduled for one-half hour or hour sessions, with the option of longer sessions. Holographic Repatterning sessions last approximately one and a half hours. I also offer forums, support groups, and weekend workshops in interspecies communication.

Glossary of Terms

Metaphysical Jargon, Simplified

When you make your appointment with your intuitive practitioner, they will describe to you their primary methods of divining information. Below is a list of common terms and their meanings to better help you, the client, understand more completely what is being offered to you.

Animal Communication: The sending and receiving of information between humans and animals.

Aroma Therapy (or Aromatherapy): The use of fragrances to facilitate a desired emotional or physical state.

Astrological Chart: The astrologer refers to a chart listing the placement of the planets and constellations as they were at your time of birth. Each astral body is said to have an influence on your character and destiny.

Aura Readings: Based on the widely held belief that your emotions set off electro-chemical vibrations which vary in frequencies. These frequencies, in turn, may be seen as different colors in the field just outside your body. The collection of colors is called your aura. Loving thoughts create higher vibrations, a physical illness creates muddy vibrations, and so forth. When a practitioner reads your aura, they are looking at the energy field you are generating and interpret the colors accordingly. (See "vibrational reading.")

Chakra: An energy center in the body.

Channeling: The intuitive relates the information from a specific entity (such as your guardian angel) or from the collective unconscious.

Clairvoyant Reading: The psychic sees in their mind's eye an image. Sometimes the image is literal, often it is allegorical. For example, they may see an image of your boss handing you a sack of gold, meaning that you are going to get a raise. In order to enhance the clarity, some practitioners will hold an object belonging to you while doing your reading. This type of clairvoyance is technically referred to as psychometry.

Energetic Healing: On the theory that energy travels along specific roads, this treatment removes "blockages" in the roadway that hinder the quick transfer of your emotional, spiritual or physical energy.

Holistic Healing: Healing all aspects of an individual: spiritual, mental, emotional, physical.

Intuitive, an: A person who has a strong sense of inner knowing. For purposes of this book, we have used the noun "intuitive" interchangeably with the nouns "psychic" or "sensitive."

Karma: Your spiritual bank account. Otherwise known as "You reap what you sow."

Karmic Healing: Healing of the soul which results in losing the need to keep practicing until you get it right.

Medium: A person who channels information from a spiritual source, usually a deceased individual. (See "Channel")

Numerology: The practitioner translates your name and/or your birthdate into a series of numbers, which they manipulate until they get a single number. Each number has its own significance, which the numerologist then relates to your present life cycle.

Palm Reading: The practitioner determines information from looking at your palm.

Past Life Regression: The practitioner helps you to recall incidents from your past lives which may have a bearing on a present-day situation.

Pendant, the use of a: The psychic has a small pendulum in his/her hand, and holds it over a series of symbols outlined on paper. The direction of the swing of the pendulum determines the answer to the questions.

Personal Transformation: A catch-all phrase describing any kind of change to your mind, body or spirit. Denotes a change for the better.

Psychic, a: An individual who possesses a strong sense of intuition.

Psychic Fair: A collection of booths from which operate a number of intuitive arts practitioners.

Reiki: A Japanese form of moving healing energy through the hands.

Sensitive, a: see "psychic" and "intuitive."

Shaman: An individual who practices an ancient method of spiritual healing based on an ability to access non-ordinary reality.

Soul Reading: A description of that part of you that lives on after death.

Spiritual Community: A collection of like-minded people whose goal is working towards the highest good for all.

Spiritual Counseling: Loving advice given to help you towards your highest good.

Spiritual Path: That series of events in our life that leads us to being closer to God, our Higher Power, or other ideal that is greater than ourselves.

Tarot the use of: The Tarot is a deck of cards, and each card displays a picture representing a thought, action or attitude. The deck is shuffled and a selection of cards laid out, and the layout is referred to as a "spread." The spread conveys information to the psychic reader, such as an answer to a particular question or an overall view of your life. There are different types of Tarot cards, the most popular being the Ryder-Waite deck.

Transformational Healing: Healing of the spirit which then results in the subsequent healing of the mind and body.

Vibrational Reading: The practitioner sees and interprets the energy surrounding your body. (see Aura Reading.)

Rev. Lori Clouden

Clairvoyant readings * Energetic healing & cleansing
Spiritual empowerment classes * Ceremonies * Counseling

Services in support of your natural state of abundance and joy

Phone: (303) 988-3950   E-Mail: LoriCloud1@aol.com

Convenient Denver Area Location

Personal guidance & energy
balancing for body, mind & spirit

Janet de Coriolis
Conscious Channel / Reiki Master
(425) 881-8481 or Stargazers (425) 885-7289

Channeled Readings   *Reiki Initiations*
Teaching/Healing Groups   *Reiki Treatments*

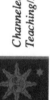

Readings - Classes

Karen Cornell
Intuitive Consulting

(206) 729-2320
(800) 421-1682
www.angelwood.com

CHANNELED ANGEL READINGS

Liz MacDonald
Workshops/Readings
9500 Roosevelt Way N.E., Suite 210
Seattle, WA 98115

206 729-2320
800 698-8985

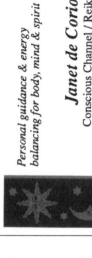

www.angelwood.com

DRAGONWOOD DESIGN

818.385.0818 PHONE
818.385.0868 Fax
dragonwoodz@earthlink.net

KAREN KROLL

Vivian

specializes in

Tools & Techniques for Self-Transformation

Psychic Readings

Past Life Regressions

Chakra and Aura Healings

Soul Healing

Transformations Unlimited

6805 SW Cherryhill Dr.
Beaverton, OR   97008

(503) 671-9041

MBI

Management by Intuition

Laurie McQuary
psychic consultant
personal business

individual • group • seminar
Voice 503/636-1832 Fax 636-1093

15800 S.W. Boones Ferry Rd.
Bd. C-205 • Lake Oswego, Oregon 97035

Marian Simon

- tarot
- soul retrieval
- shamanic healing

(503) 831-0158

P.O. BOX 275
DALLAS, OR 97338

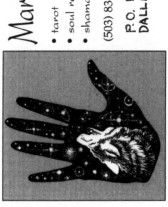

Word Magic

Sheryl L. Mehary

1655 S. Elm St, #517
Canby, Oregon 97013
E-mail: smehary@aol.com
Fax: 503-263-2438
Phone: 503-263-2437

Turning your thoughts, ideas and words into creative professional documents, projects and books.